S0-BSN-389

Romain Goldron

BYZANTINE AND MEDIEVAL MUSIC

H. S. Stuttman Company, Inc., Publishers
Distributed by Doubleday & Company, Inc.

Designed by Erik Nitsche

Copyright © 1968 H. S. Stuttman Co., Inc.
All rights reserved
Copyright © 1966 Editions Rencontre

HISTORY
OF
MUSIC

2

1 *Musician playing a portable organ.*
(Late 13th century)

1

Contents

2 At Byzantium, Jewish, Syrian and Greek traditions become integrated into the new Christianity. These panels from a Byzantine casket show dancers with tabors, revealing Greek influence at work. (4th century)

Birth of a Church and a Liturgy

Although the actual beginnings of Christian music have remained buried in the mists of time, its early forms of expression were clearly the outcome of experiment and assimilation. Like Christianity itself, the music it was to develop had to feel its way, so to speak, along unknown paths.

In the early days of the Church, singers turned for inspiration to a number of contemporary sources and traditions—Hebrew, Greek, Syrian and Roman, Celtic and others, to a lesser degree—and it was on these that they drew for the elementary principles of their newborn liturgy. It was just the same for early Christian painters, for, beset as they were with exactly similar problems of form, they made use of the iconographic symbols of existing traditions.

It is no secret, for instance, that the "Good Shepherd" theme was taken from a small statue from Tanagra, a town in ancient Attica. This statue showed Mercury, messenger of the gods, bearing a goat in his arms. Similarly, at first, Christ bore a distinct resemblance to Apollo, and the beard to which we are accustomed was missing. Many other examples could be given to support the conclusion that the many and varied elements music borrowed from divers sources did not blend into one

BRIDWELL LIBRARY
SOUTHERN METHODIST UNIVERSITY
DALLAS, TEXAS   75222

3 Orpheus with his lyre. The legend of Orpheus symbolized the magic forces of music, and was to find great favor with Western musicians, from Monteverdi to Glück and Stravinsky. (Mosaic from Jerusalem—Roman era)

4-5 *Following pages.*
Instrumental music was practiced
at the court of Constantine,
but none of it has survived.
The tabor and the viol can be
recognized on this icon in
popular 16th century style.
(Byzantine Museum, Athens)

harmonious whole all at once any more than was the case with Christian art. One more thing is certain. There was in this liturgy, which was essentially vocal, a built-in determination that it should be the very antithesis of Roman music as practiced in the decadent society of the capital and other important centers of the Empire.

It has been said that Christianity took its ethics from Judea, its theology from Greece, and its organization from Rome. In the shaping of Christian music these three sources were no less active. The fact that many melodies were taken over from the synagogue is logical enough, for the synagogue constituted the pattern on which the Church was organizing itself. Yet the first texts which the Fathers of the Church devoted to music reveal traces of Pythagoras and Plato rather than Jewish influence. To the Greek mind, we should remember, music was part and parcel of a mathematical philosophy. Finally, when it came to the orderly integration of so many different elements, Rome was the predominant influence.

Ethnically speaking, after about A.D. 100 Rome was virtually an Eastern city. All reference to the history of the Christian community in the capital soon takes away whatever surprise one might feel at the manifold influences which this community assimilated and, with the passage of time,

changed into something else. Indeed, surprise would only be justified if this were not the case. As early as A.D. 187, the Bishop of Lyon, St. Iranaeus, who was martyred in the year 202, was already listing some twenty different kinds of Christianity;[1] and doctrine, as yet ill-defined, was subject to a ceaseless flow of new ideas. During the political and spiritual chaos that followed the fall of the Empire, Christianity fell back upon this great reserve for the strength and vigor which enabled it to keep alive the tradition to which it was heir; and in that spent and exhausted world, it managed to lay the foundations of a new civilization in which there was to be an unexpected and unforeseen development of music.

It was not long before the influence of Rome became preponderant in the Church. The first converts were frequently either slaves or members of the middle or lower classes. As such they were people who had every reason to resent a society that oppressed or ill-used them. They were instinctively opposed in every respect to the customs, habits, morals and tastes of the ruling and privileged classes. They sublimated the hardships and miseries imposed on them from outside and transformed them into active spiritual values. Christianity helped them to regain some vestige of human dignity. Living as they were in the midst of a most

NOEMBRЫ. Z

4

ΑϹΚ

5

6 *Ceremonial at the Byzantine court reflects the pomp and ritual of Eastern courts in general. Any public appearance of the Emperor was surrounded with great magnificence and ceremony. Theodosius I (346-395), victor over the Goths and a convert to Christianity, can be seen on a raised dais, surrounded by the members of his court. It can be assumed, from the presence of a portable organ, that the figures below the platform are singers. (Column to Theodosius, Hippodrome, Constantinople—4th century)*

dissolute society, they imposed on themselves a rule of life which was all the more severe because of the licentiousness that surrounded them.

This explains the antipathy on the part of early Christians to instrumental music, for this was a feature of Roman junketings in the amphitheatre and in the circus, with its great hydraulic organs. As long as the melodies they adopted, no matter from what source, differed from those figuring in the rich man's orgies or in the entertainment of the Neros, it is highly probable that they cared very little about their actual origin. So carefully did the Christians guard the music they had acquired from all taint of decadent Roman art that they even denied it the support of the cithara (an enlarged version of the lyre). For them, right from the start, music was intrinsically bound up with the aims of their religion and the destiny of the Church. They could have had no inkling, those early Christians, of the great untrodden ways into which the Christian code would direct the art of sound. Later, when music that had been purely vocal came to join forces with instrumental music, it was mature enough to impose its principles on it, and there came into being an art completely unlike any that had been known before, either in the ancient world or in the great civilizations of the East. References to music are to be found in even the earliest literary records, and at no known period does the world seem to have been without it. But the music we know today is the development of only a few centuries.

Psalms and Hymns

What was it they sang, these first Christians? Of what did their liturgy consist? The Office of the Hours, which they borrowed from Jewish ritual, is generally acknowledged to have been the first element. This was, in effect, the singing of psalms, or perhaps we should say, the modulated recitation of psalms, for it was already the 9th century before a rudimentary notation made its appearance. Inasmuch as they adopted certain acclamatory words, such as "Alleluia" and "Amen," it seems probable, too, that the Christians also imitated traditional lines of melody. It is interesting to recall that Biblical psalms reveal a strong link with Sumerian hymns; and when the assembled faithful were entrusted with the task of punctuating the soloist's chant with an alleluia—or a brief chorus with a fixed melody, responsorial psalmody (alternation between soloist and choir) was introduced into the Church. Actually, the Christians were adopting a form of liturgy that had been practiced in Mesopotamia and Egypt.

... erum uidebo uos alleluia et gaudebit cor uestrum et gaudium uestrum nemo ...

... Modicum uidebitur me quia uado ad patrem et iterum uidebitis me et gaudebit cor uestrum ...

... loquutus est dominus discipulis suis dicens ascendo ad patrem meum et ad patrem uestrum ...

OFFICIVM INDIE ASCENSIONIS DNI AD VESPERVM

Alle ...

... nante deo alleluia alle ...

... Psallite domino psallite ... deo nostro alleluia ...

... qui ascendit super celos celorum ad orientem ...

... uocem suam uocem uirtutis sue ... e alleluia ...

... rector caeli auctor potest magnificentia e ...

... nubis habitacio e ... sus suum ... trum qui ponit nubem ...

... incommutabilis sermus deus nostri ... incons ... prehensibilis ...

... gaudia cordetur angelo ... rum cum gratia ... qua ascendit de nubibus ...

9

7-8 Previous pages.
From the 4th century the Christian churches
were occupied with the development of
coherent liturgies; the Ambrosian rite
of Milan, the Roman, the Gallican (the Church
in France), the Mozarabic (Spanish Christianity
under Moorish domination). The latter
was due to Archbishop Leander of Seville.
It is to this liturgy that the
antiphonaries belong—books containing
the various parts of the Office.
(Leon Cathedral—10th century)
9 Psalter in uncial writing
(large letters used in Ancient Greek and
Latin writing). Frontispiece shows
King David with his lawyers and musicians
with horns and trumpets. He is engaged
in writing psalms. (English School
illumination—Canterbury—8th century)

The prototype of the *psalm,* then, is to be found in Jewish worship, but the spiritual origin of the *hymn* is Greek and Syrian. The hymn is a free composition based on texts not taken direct from Scripture. It is in verse form, each verse being sung to the same tune, and it relies on regular rhythm.[2] In the 4th century, in Asia Minor, hymn-singing was still accompanied by clapping of hands and dance movements.

It was not long, moreover, before vocalized singing appeared in the liturgy, in the form of the *jubilus.* In simple terms, vocalization consisted of melodic extensions of vowel sounds (for instance, the "a" at the end of alleluia), and for a definition of *jubilus* we cannot do better than turn to St. Augustine, Bishop of Hippo (354-430), the greatest of the Latin Fathers:

"He who sings a jubilus uses no words; he expresses his joy in inarticulate sound. His heart is overwhelmed with joy and mere words no longer suffice. He lets himself go in a cry of happiness too great for words."[3]

This kind of singing almost certainly came into the Church from two sources at one and the same time—the Jewish practice of cantillation and the mystical chants and songs used by gnostic sects. Gnosticism was one of the early heresies, which sought to combine Christian beliefs with others de-rived from Greek or Oriental sources. Indeed, the very fact that these vocalizations were, in the main, performed upon a word that was foreign and a chant of Hebrew origin—the Alleluia—is in itself significant.[4]

Eastern influence, therefore, was unmistakably apparent in the infant Church. Greek was the language used in the liturgy at first, as the "Kyrie Eleison" reminds us even in present times. The formation of a Latin liturgy began with the 3rd century.

Byzantium

In the year 313, Emperor Constantine promulgated the Edict of Milan, which conceded to "Christians and all others the freedom to practice the religion of their choice." In the year 330, the Emperor was to turn his back on Rome and found a new city at Byzantium. He called this city the "New Rome," though later it was to be renamed Constantinople. This momentous Edict of Milan enabled the Christian Church to emerge from the shadows and to publicly proclaim its authority.

Great was the historical importance of Constantine's decision to transfer the Imperial capital. Byzantium grew and developed in an amazing fashion. There, far better than it could have done

17

10

in the decadent atmosphere of Rome, Greek tradition could merge into the new world which was taking shape under the impetus of Christian ideas. Byzantium became the center of art and culture, of philosophy and mysticism. History was preparing Byzantium's place as the guardian of all ancient culture; and it occupied a privileged position at the crossroads where the old Mediterranean civilizations met those of the Orient.

It is not easy to assess accurately the extent to which Byzantine influence affected music. It is only in recent times that we have succeeded in deciphering its system of notation. When more precise and detailed information about Byzantine music becomes available, it will doubtless be possible to determine more exactly the nature of the "continuous musical current emanating from the East" which Combarieu observed and which he considered a general and important factor.[5]

Byzantine Music and Art

If there is in existence an art that merits the description "abstract" (a term so wrongly used today), it is Byzantine art, utterly opposed as it is to the matter-of-fact realism of Roman painting and sculpture. A veritable abyss separates Byzantine and Roman concepts of art. Byzantine art is hieratic—sacred, priestly; it is a vehicle for ideas and truths of a supernatural order. Everything in the way of action, poses, choice of colors, etc., is fixed in accordance with certain standards of symbolism. Impassive and haughty in its spell-binding grandeur and power, it is the reflection of a world of divine concepts and divine models.

In architecture—religious architecture, that is—Byzantium made effective use of the cupola or the throne; it featured not Christ crucified, but Christ risen and triumphant. For one of the best examples, we cannot do better than point to St. Sophia itself. Built by Justinian, Emperor in the 6th century, it was designed to be the finest building in the world. When the Emperor saw the completed basilica, he exclaimed: "Glory be to God, who has thought me worthy to complete this work! Solomon, I have outdone thee!" After the fall of the city, St. Sophia became a mosque; today it is a museum.

This grandiose, hieratic style was reflected in the lavish pomp of the court, which recalled the splendid Oriental pomp of Assyrian and Babylonian palaces. The Emperor was both absolute monarch and high priest, and his public appearances were attended by full and magnificent ritual. When, with the Empress and the princes and the patriarch, he made his way to St. Sophia, he was accompanied

10 One type of four-sided psalter.
(9th century)
11 Another kind of cithara. Played with
a bow, this instrument was widely
used in Wales. (9th century)

11

by a procession punctuating his progress with liturgical songs (consisting of acclamation and response).

Like the mosaic artist, or the painter, it was not for the Byzantine musician to devise new tunes for the hymns. His brief was to conform to traditional patterns, for these were regarded as direct inspirations from the angels. Earthly music, at best, was but the echo of the Seraphim praising God; the musician, therefore, was well content to embellish or vary the angelic pattern.

The chief forms of Byzantine Christian music were the psalm, the hymn and the canon. In all these, Byzantine hieraticism is combined with great richness of style. Thus the hymn, providing ample opportunity for development, engendered a new form, the *kontakion,* a kind of poetic homily comprising twenty or thirty verses (6th and 7th centuries). A master in this field was Romano, a native of Syria, in the 6th century.

The canon, which succeeded the kontakion, comprised nine odes designed to replace the nine canticles of the Morning Office, each short ode having four verses. The composer whose name has always been associated with the canon is Andrew, Metropolitan of Gortyne, in Crete, who died A.D. 740. His "Grand Canon" had 250 verses. Byzantine liturgy also made great use of additional single verses which could either precede or conclude a more important piece, like the canon, but were sometimes inserted into the main piece.

It should be noted that the basis of both Byzantine liturgy and Latin liturgy is Greek, Syrian and primitive Hebrew. There is, of course, a reminder of Byzantine liturgy to be found in the music of the Greek Orthodox Church.

Court Music

The magnificence and pomp of the Imperial court made demands on music no less exacting than those of the Church. The hymns that were sung in honor of the Emperor were not in reality very different from choruses and hymns sung in church. A feature of these hymns was singing in dialogue, a custom dating back to the Church of Antioch. The choir was divided in two parts. One group clad in blue sang facing another clad in green. These colors, it is certain, had some significance— they are to be found together in many of the Ravenna mosaics. The singing was accompanied by two silver organs. St. Mark's in Venice seems to have possessed two similar silver organs.[6] It is hardly possible to believe that the vocal and instrumental music, with two choirs, which developed there, with the Gabrieli, was a mere accident; for

19

12

13

Venice, by virtue of the nature and direction of its trade, was always in close touch with the East. Andrea Gabrieli (1510-1586) and Giovanni Gabrieli (1557-1612) were uncle and nephew, and they composed a considerable amount of vocal and instrumental music for double choirs.

Instrumental music, with flutes, trumpets and cymbals, was also performed at the Byzantine court, though none of this has survived. The musicians used to play Persian style, hidden away behind drapes.

Influences on Western Music

Byzantine influence on Western music cannot be traced as clearly as it can in painting. The reason for this is that we are acquainted only with the music of the Latin liturgy in the form it assumed when a system of notation made it possible to commit its outlines to writing. We are well aware of the great influence of Byzantium on our plastic arts, from Cimabué right through to Duccio (1260-1320). Like the other painters of Siena, they did not break completely with the earlier Byzantine tradition, as Giotto did, but tried instead—and tried successfully—to breathe new life into the old Byzantine forms.

There is no reason to suppose that music alone would remain untouched by the same Byzantine influence. It was almost certainly the example of Byzantium that induced the Latin Fathers to relax, to some extent, their primitive and hostile attitude toward music, which was thought by many people to be incompatible with true faith. As late as the 5th century, there were those who thought with Bruno Carthus:

"God does not like music for itself; He has no more need of it than He has of human sacrifice. . . ." "If He allows us to sing, or desires us to sing," says this author, seemingly so well informed as to what God wanted yet so much at odds with all the priests of antiquity and the Orient, "it is out of pity for Man's frailty and his predilection for childish things. . . ." In the 2nd century, Tertullian was writing: "Musical concerts with viol and lute belong to Apollo, to the Muses, to Minerva and Mercury, who invented them; ye who are Christians, hate and abhor these things whose very authors themselves must be the object of loathing and aversion." (*De Spectaculis, X.*)

The doubt and uncertainty into which more narrow-minded souls were plunged by this problem of music in worship is evidenced by an oft-quoted text from St. Augustine's *Confessions*. "Sometimes," says the Saint, "because I am ever on the watch for a snare of some kind, I am falsely led into exag-

20

12 St. John Chrysostom (347-407).
He introduced antiphonal chant
(alternating chant) at Constantinople.
(from a 16th century stamp)
13 Boethius (480-525), Minister to
Theodoric II at Ravenna and eminent theorist
and philosopher. As a result of his
tractates, Greek musical theory was to
permeate the whole of the Middle Ages.
Boethius fell into disgrace and
was beheaded. (16th century stamp)
14 Georgius Pachymerus (1242-1310),
eminent Byzantine theorist and
philosopher. (16th century woodcut)

gerated severity; and then all I want is to shield the ears of all Christians, and mine own also, from all sound of those sweet tunes which accompany the Psalms of David . . . ; and yet, when I remember how I wept in the early days of my conversion as I listened to the songs of the Church, and when I remember too how now also I am moved not by the song but by what it expresses . . . then I can appreciate anew the value of such an institution. I am therefore inclined to look favorably on the maintenance of this custom, though I do not claim to settle the matter; yet it would seem that through the joys of hearing, the fainting soul can grow firmer in piety."[7]

We do not find the same reservation in texts from the Eastern Empire. Their authors, nurtured on Greek philosophy, managed to incorporate the doctrines of Pythagoras and the disciples of Plato into the religion of Christ most successfully. Important in this connection is a treatise by Denis, Bishop of Athens, who was martyred in the 1st century. It sheds considerable light on the concepts of Byzantium. In this same century, St. Ignatius of Antioch is supposed to have had a vision of angelic choirs praising God, singing alternately, and he lost no time in putting this vision into effect in his church. St. John Chrysostom (347-407) sums up in essence for us when he declares: "Music was

14

15-16 St. Ambrose (340-397), Bishop of Milan. The popular hymn and its ensuing success can be attributed to him. They were composed as a means of keeping the people occupied when the Bishop, persecuted by the Empress Justina, shut himself up in his church with the faithful. They are known as Ambrosian hymns and are still preserved in Milan in a special rite. (raised prints—16th century)

15

invented in Heaven, which resounds with the song of the Heavenly Hosts; our singing is nought but an echo, an imitation of the songs the angels sing."

These ideas gradually filtered through into the West, providing painters with one of their favorite themes and inspirations. From the singing angels of Fra Angelico to the concert of angels of Matthias Grünewald (the German painter, *ca.* 1460-1528), musical art—like painting—found the theme of angelic song a never-ending source of inspiration. It may well be that we owe our music to these angels of Byzantium.

Byzantine influence did not cease with the fall of Constantinople, captured by the Turks in 1453. Scholars and philosophers from Constantinople sought refuge in the West, and when the Renaissance dawned they were to prove a leavening force, especially in Florence under the Medicis.[8]

St. Ambrose

After the Edict of Milan, which had enabled Christianity to come forth from the catacombs, the Latin Church, too, introduced antiphonal psalmody into its liturgy. Whereas in the responsorial form the congregation used to be limited to interpolations into the chant of the soloist here and there, now the faithful were divided into two equal choirs, singing alternately and then joining for the chorus, which was called the Antiphon. According to St. Augustine, this innovation was due to Saint Ambrose: "During his persecution by the Empress Justina, the Bishop took shelter with the faithful in the Church at Milan, and to keep the people occupied, he made them sing hymns and psalms in the Eastern manner." (*Confessions IX.*) It seems unlikely that an innovation of this nature would have been introduced into an environment so athirst for supernatural truths and sacred legends unless its spiritual and theological justification included reference of some kind to the angelic choirs of Heaven.

Soon, however, in spite of the fact that the growing Christian sect had been careful to steer clear of anything that might have been reminiscent of pagan Roman music, it was forced by circumstances, as a matter of religious policy, to allow some concessions. Some of the gnostic sects had conceived the ingenious idea of "putting their subversive ideas into couplets." This musical propaganda undeniably met with success. The Christians found that by itself theology was powerless against this enemy, and decided that there was no alternative but to use the same weapon themselves. It was St. Ephraim who first tried out these tactics against heretics in Eastern Syria.

16

17

18

*17   St. Sylvester, Pope from 314 to 335.
18   St. Hilary, Bishop of Poitiers
(303?-367). He composed hymns with
popular tunes like those he had heard
during his exile in the East.
19   Pope St. Gregory (540-604).
To him is attributed the reform and
organization of liturgical singing,
whence the term "Gregorian chant"
given to plain-chant. (from a
Breviary belonging to the Duchess
of Milan—16th century)*

St. Hilary, Bishop of Poitiers in the 4th century, was exiled to Phrygia for a time, and on his return he tried to use the same methods as St. Ephraim, though he was singularly unsuccessful. St. Ambrose, in Milan, was more fortunate. He composed numerous hymns with popular tunes and lively rhythm. These became known as Ambrosian hymns and are still preserved, in a special rite, in the Church of Milan.[10]

Milan was not the only church that took steps, under the guidence of St. Ambrose, to work out a coherent liturgy. In the 4th century, at least three other liturgies were taking shape: the Roman, the Gallican and the Mozarabic. Archbishop Leander of Seville was responsible for the last-named. This same century was to see the creation of the first *Schola Cantorum* in Rome, under the aegis of Sylvester I, a saint of the Church and Pope from 314 to 355.

Gregorian Chant

Gregorian chant is sometimes called plain-chant. It refers to the musical repertory of the Christian Church as it was developed between the 5th and 9th centuries.

Why "plain-chant"? The term arose because authors in the Middle Ages wished to differentiate between the *planus cantus,* or unified chant, and the *cantus mensuratus,* or melody with measurable rhythm, in common use in polyphony and singing.

Why "Gregorian"? This is because St. Gregory the Great—the Pope from 590 to 604—is regarded as having organized and codified the miscellany of melodies in use by church singers. He laid down "catholic" principles, that is, a set of universal rules, for the music of the liturgy. In the various regions, which were often a law unto themselves, there was a great deal of variation.

Gregory came from noble Roman stock. After studying the liberal arts, he became Prefect of Rome. When he was about thirty, he became a monk. He turned his home into a Benedictine monastery and became Abbot; and he wrote a life of St. Benedict, some of whose first followers he had known. Among other things, the Abbot was responsible for the liturgy and its direction, and at this stage in his life Gregory was closely concerned with the music of the Church.

The Pope of the time, ·Pelagus II, sent Gregory as Legate to Constantinople. He was there seven years, time enough to become familiar with the rich music of Byzantine liturgy. When he returned to Rome, he was elected Pope. It was Gregory who was to undertake the conversion of England, after he had been moved to pity by the sight of English

24

S · GREGORIVS

VRELS ꞏ ROMAE ꞏ EPIS ꞏ COP

19

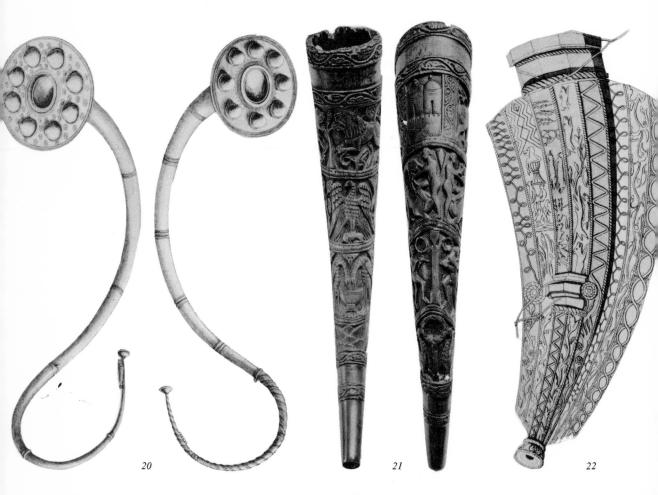

20 *21* *22*

26

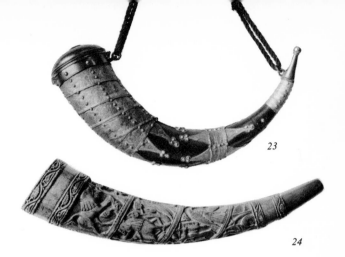

20 Scandinavian instruments
(Bronze Age); primitive horn-type
instrument, usually discovered
and unearthed in pairs, hence
one supposes that they were used
by two people for signaling.
21-24 Small horn said to
be that of Gaston de Béarn,
seen from different sides.
22 Ancient Danish horn.
Its decoration is displayed.
23 Hunting horn. (9th century—
Cathedral Treasury, Maestricht)

23

24

children in a Roman slave market. He died before he could complete his missionary journey to England, and he entrusted the mission to a group of monks during the closing years of the 6th century.

Although plain-chant came to be called after Gregory, and although there are in existence miniatures that show Gregory tracing neumes—"with a dove, symbol of the Holy Ghost, pecking his ear—" [11] he never actually composed anything. We are familiar with the official documents of Gregory's reign, and there is no mention of music in them. It was not until three centuries after his death that people began to talk of "Gregorian chant."

It would be useless to labor the extent to which Gregory was responsible for the ordering of the liturgy. It matters little whether he was the instigator or the author, or whether he was merely credited with the work because he was "all things to all men" and greatly loved. What is important is that the work was achieved by someone, with far-reaching results.

From that time on, the Church possessed an Antiphonary, a complete collection of liturgical music. It contained music for all the different religious exercises classified according to the ecclesiastical year, with instructions as to the manner in which it was to be performed. The Antiphonary, it is said, was placed on the altar of St. Peter's and

secured by a golden chain.[12] At the same time, a reorganization of the Schola Cantorum made it the vital hub of official liturgy. Later on, Charles the Great consolidated Gregory's work, for he decreed that Roman chant was to be used by the Franks, although it must be said that his reasons were political rather than musical.

Gregorian chant, invariably monodic, is based on the Greek diatonic scale, and its modes, too, were adopted from the Greek, though it changed the starting point in the scale. There is a difference between the recitative or intoned chant and the melodic or embellished chant. The former—which is also called syllabic (its syllables being intoned on the same note)—is reserved for the reading of Epistles, Gospels, psalms and prayers. The second is used in the execution of antiphons, hymns and singing at Mass.

However, while there is no doubt that the author or authors of Gregorian reform were competent administrators, they successfully destroyed any initiative there might have been, and in practice they invariably opposed anything new in the way of composition.

One may well wonder, as does Jacques Chailley,[13] whether the refined, subtle Gregorian of the *scholae* is the same, really, as that which the contemporaries of Chilperic knew. Is this admirable yet schol-

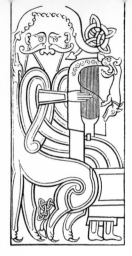

25

arly form of art the same as that which existed at the time of the last of the Merovingians, who ruled France between 500 and 750? "Both the theory and the subsequent notation show signs of grace notes, trills, shakes, melting vowels and a thousand and one embellishments which would scandalize present-day apostles of tradition. . . . Certain pieces were meant for solo-singing and when these were vocalized they must have been very like that intoxicating virtuosity of voice which was to be, much later, and in a different form, a feature of Italian opera."

Charles-Albert Cingria (1883–1954) said: "Gregorian chant is much more in harmony with the *Bel canto* of Milan than with pointed arches." He added, quite unafraid of dashing preconceived ideas: "Gregorian art is never more at home than in the setting of baroque architecture, for it is meant for the soloist; it is an art of vocalizations and trills, and its setting must be wild and extravagant baroque like that found nowhere outside South America, where the shape of living beings or things ceases to be recognizable."

Cingria saw baroque as a Syrian-Roman revival. Chailley makes a further point about the way in which words have changed their meaning: today we use the word "ecstasy," in defiance of its etymology, to describe the moment when a devotee turns inward, into himself, in his joy—the very moment, in fact, when in other ages he was said to "give out" and emerge from himself in noisy and rhythmic exaltation. In his letter to the Corinthians, St. Paul wrote: "I commend those gatherings of the faithful where, as a result of the mass excitement built up by the singing, they rise to their feet, 'outside themselves' so to speak, to improvise. . . ." though in fairness to the Apostle, he did add a request that this should be done in an orderly manner.

"The heated arguments put forward by both sides in the dispute concerning music as a means of worship are almost incomprehensible if one thinks of plain-chant as unequivocally inward and contemplative. They do, however, make sense if one thinks of it as a passionate and exalting song of ecstasy." Moreover, the study of music continues to reveal further links between plain-chant and the chant of the Yemenite Jews or that of the Byzantines, whose lusty vocalizations betokened a frenetic lyricism. It is known that at Auxerre, in the 13th century, the canons of the cathedral used to throw a ball—the *pilotta*—to each other in time to the music; that at Limoges they used to dance in the choir of St. Leonard's, singing as they did so, "St. Martial, pray for us and we will dance for you." (St. Martial was Bishop of Limoges sometime dur-

25 Irish miniature (8th century) showing King David playing the harp. Although ousted by other instruments, the harp has retained in Ireland a glorious past and goes back to prehistoric times.
26 Harpists. (12th century— entrance to Abbey of St. Denis, Seine)

25 Irish miniature (8th century) showing King David playing the harp. Although ousted by other instruments, the harp has retained in Ireland a glorious past and goes back to prehistoric times.
26 Harpists. (12th century— entrance to Abbey of St. Denis, Seine)

ing the 3rd century.) Again, at Sens, even in the middle of the 13th century, the precentor, next in rank below the Bishop, used to dance in the nave to the sound of a Gregorian chant,[14] his sacred ring upon his finger and his staff of office in his left hand. One is reminded of David, dancing in front of the Ark of the Covenant.

We should be careful—and the facts and events referred to have precisely this aim in view—to remove the distorting spectacles of our modern rationalism before we examine the centuries that have gone before. We should do well to remember, too, that the golden age of Gregorian coincided with a most confused and disturbed period in European history. While the Church was extending northward, step by step, a tidal wave of humanity was sweeping down upon the south, and it was from their encounter that European civilization would be born. Christianity held fast against the cyclone, the onrushing maelstrom of races and tongues, of morals, ideas and customs. In all truth, this was no time for academic traditions or art for art's sake. It is nothing short of a miracle that a musical tradition like Gregorian could have developed at all under such conditions. The fact that it did develop is proof enough of its strength and vigor.

All European music sprang from this source; indeed, musicians from Luther to Bach and Berlioz

26

27

would return time and time again to this same spring for refreshment and inspiration.

Profane Music

What of pagan music? It would be a mistake to think it had died out. Invaders who swept westward had their music, although we know exceedingly little about it. It undoubtedly existed. The word "barbarian" does not necessarily imply "savage." Gonzague de Reynold, in *The Celts,* (1949),[15] demonstrates clearly how very near the Celts came to achieving, together with the Latins and Greeks, a third great people in the ancient world, and how very near they came to civilization. It would be impossible to overestimate the great influence of Celtic bards on the poetry of Europe.

The Germans, too, had a poetry of their own, and possessed their epic and mythological songs, which they passed on by word of mouth. When their warriors went forth to battle it was their custom to sing hymns to Thor, the god of thunder.[16]

The Roman "mime" continued for a long time. The use of instruments had by no means ceased, despite the fact that the Church forbade them. Can one really believe that this music, which was not written down and about which we know nothing, would exert no influence at all? Nothing is further from the truth. It was not long before the music emerged from its limbo to impart the freshness and richness of its popular character to the music of scholars.

In spite of their military anxieties, Frankish kings clamored for musicians. "We are sending you the poet and cithara player you asked for," wrote Theodoric, who reigned in Ravenna from 455 to 526, in reply to Clovis, king of the Franks. "He is skilled at his art. May he bring you joy as he acclaims your might and your glory with vibrating strings and harmonious voice."

This same Theodoric had among his ministers Boethius, poet, statesman and philosopher (born in Rome in 480), and Cassiodorous, the philosopher who succeeded Boethius in office when he was beheaded. It was thanks to Boethius in particular that Greek and Pythagoran musical theory was handed down to the Middle Ages, to furnish scholars of that time with unlimited food for thought.

All this was happening in the 6th century.

Historians are agreed that the two hundred years that followed represent the very darkest period in Western history. Spiritual life was nonexistent outside the monasteries; it seemed, for a while, as if Christianity itself would be swept away under the onslaught of new invaders—the Saracens. Spain

27 Stave written on Guidonian hand from Perego, "La Regolo del Canto," 1622.
28 Guidonian hand, from the same work.
29 Relation between notes and finger joints. The Guidonian hand, so called after Guido d'Arezzo (945?-1050?) to whom it is ascribed, always represented the left hand and was placed in all schools as a universal indicator and in elementary musical works. (Kirscher, Musurgia Universalis, 1650)

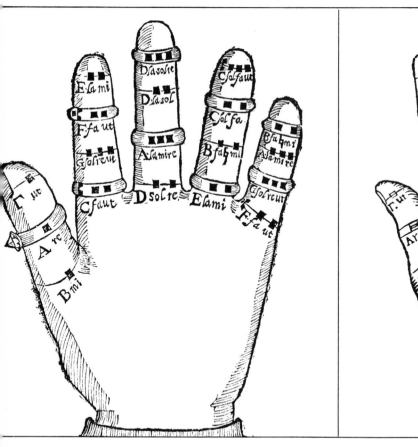

28

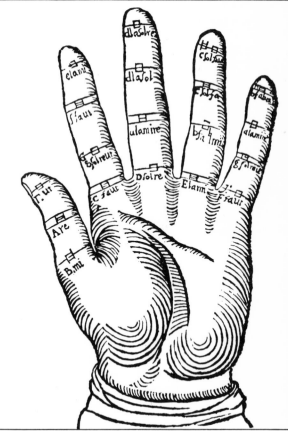

29

31

30 *Renaud de Montauban, knight-errant, hero of "The Four Sons of Aimon"*
by the Italian poet Arioste (1474-1533). Among the figures in this illumination,
one can see lute and harp players. (15th century)
31 *Psalter from Würzburg-Ebrach. Initial "B"; many instruments: organ, bells,*
ivory horn, flute, stringed instruments and instruments for bows. (early 13th century)
32 *Psalter from Bamberg. Initial "B"; instruments which were plucked*
or stroked: harps, lyre, psaltery, viol. (early 13th century)

was already submerged when the advance of Islam was brought to a halt by the victory of Charles Martel at the Battle of Poitiers in 732.

Neumes and the Development of Notation

It is difficult to understand why the Christian Church, having borrowed so many elements from Greek music, did not also make use of its system of alphabetical notation. The reason for this has never, as yet, been discovered.[17]

But the fact remains. There was no question of notation in the West before the 9th century. From then on, however, particularly in the 10th century, numerous manuscripts are to be found covered with musical signs called "neumes." "These signs," says the expert A. Machabey, "raise many problems whose bibliography alone would fill book upon book." Even the word "neume" itself has occasioned considerable discussion. It is generally agreed today that the word is simply the direct translation of the Greek *neuma*, which meant "a sign" (a sign of head or hand), and this interpretation would fit in with the belief that the neume was the written version of the signs used by the Egyptians to guide their musicians. Or, again, it could be translated as "slope"—a word that might have been used to indicate various movements of

the voice between "high" and "low." A fact that continues to fascinate the scholars is that in the oldest of the manuscripts which bear neumes a complete and co-ordinated system is immediately obvious, suggesting either a lengthy period of incubation or the adoption of an already developed scheme.[18]

It is probable, though this cannot be proved, that the neume system originated in Byzantium. The problem is complicated by the absence of any Byzantine musical score for the period between the 3rd and the 9th centuries. Could it be that during this time the chief way in which the liturgy was transmitted was by word of mouth? The looting of libraries and the burning down of many monasteries at the time when argument raged concerning the use of pictures and images in worship may explain the disappearance of relevant manuscripts.

One thing is certain. Contact between Byzantium and the West was never severed. We have already mentioned Gregory's long stay in Byzantium. Later on, there were also mutual exchanges between Pepin the Short (714-768, king of the Franks and father of Charlemagne) and Constantine Copronyme, who died in 775. The West owes its first organ to this association—apart, that is, from the Roman hydraulic organs, about which virtually nothing is known. Indeed, at one time, Charle-

32

33

33 Ornamental letter (Omega) from the St. Andrew Bible, Salzburg School. In the center, a figure with stringed instrument and bow.
34 11th century neumes, transcribed onto stave. The neume is a note symbol representing one or more sounds in the writing of plain-chant.

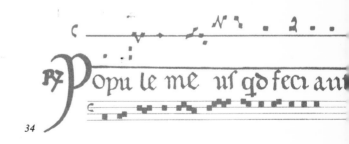

34

magne was toying with the idea of asking for the hand of the Empress Irene. Charlemagne, who later became the legendary hero of *The Song of Roland,* was also in touch with the great Arab sultan Haroun-el-Raschid, hero of the *Arabian Nights.*

Neumes were placed over each syllable of the text, resembling a kind of shorthand. The variously shaped neumes were really an aid to memory for those who knew their music well, for they only indicated the direction of the voice. They showed neither the intervals nor the precise pitch, and on these points singers received verbal instructions. The *virga* (upward dash) and the *punctus* (downward sloping dash) were the chief elements of a system which in any case had many regional variations. The punctus was ultimately replaced by a dot.

By the end of the 9th century, after the introduction of first one horizontal line and then others, the actual pitch of more and more notes was definitely shown, and this gradually developed into the five-line stave as we know it. Musicians had come to realize, however, that progress was impossible unless some way could be found to record musical thought on paper so that it could be accurately reproduced. Necessity brought about the invention, by Franco of Cologne, of a set of signs to represent notes of the various time values. These derived their shape from the earlier neumes and were gradually modified until they assumed the form of our modern notation.

The year 1000 produced a highly important figure, Guido d'Arezzo, perhaps the most significant figure in the history of music. Guido's actual birth date is not known, but he died in 1050. He divided the scale into six tones, *ut, re, mi, fa, sol* and *la,* and by subdividing his hand according to this hexachord, the leader of a choir could give his singers accurate instructions. They were now able to sing unfamiliar tunes at sight. The time they had formerly required to learn their art was considerably shortened.

We can see that Guido's idea was the basis of our solfeggio. The origin of the names he gave to his notes is interesting. He took the first syllables of each line of a famous hymn, thus—*UT quant laxis—REsonare fibris—MIra gestorum—FAmuli tuorus—SOLvi polluti—LAbii restum—Sancte Iohannes* ("Forgive, Oh St. John, the erring lips of thine unworthy servant, so that the wonder of thy deeds may find echo in hearts that wait upon thee!") The first six lines give six of the names, and by joining the *S* and the *I* of the last line, one gets *SI.*[19]

37

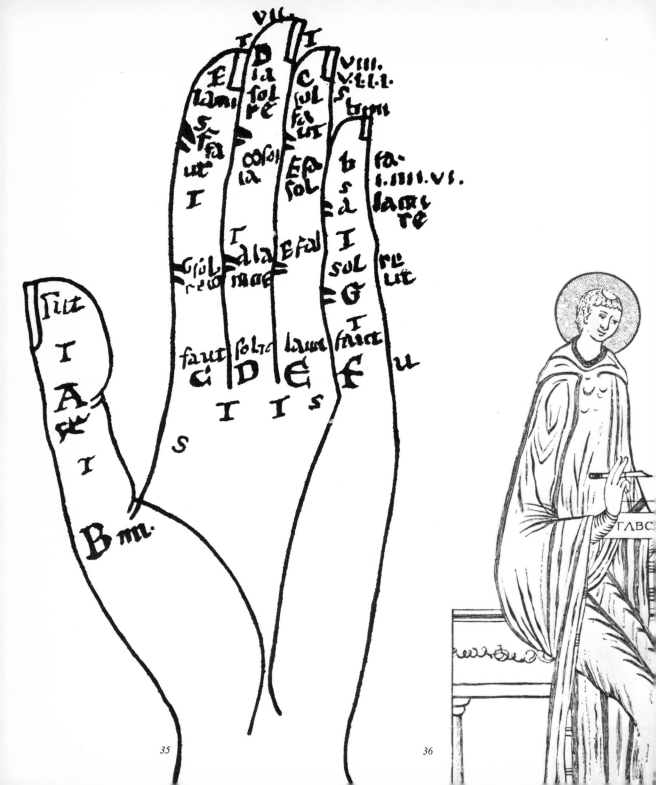

35   36

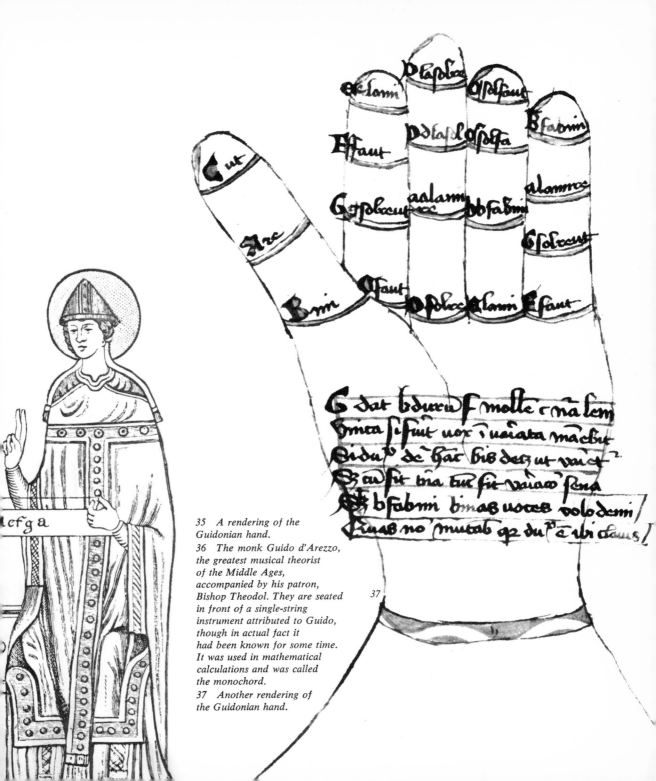

35 A rendering of the Guidonian hand.

36 The monk Guido d'Arezzo, the greatest musical theorist of the Middle Ages, accompanied by his patron, Bishop Theodol. They are seated in front of a single-string instrument attributed to Guido, though in actual fact it had been known for some time. It was used in mathematical calculations and was called the monochord.

37 Another rendering of the Guidonian hand.

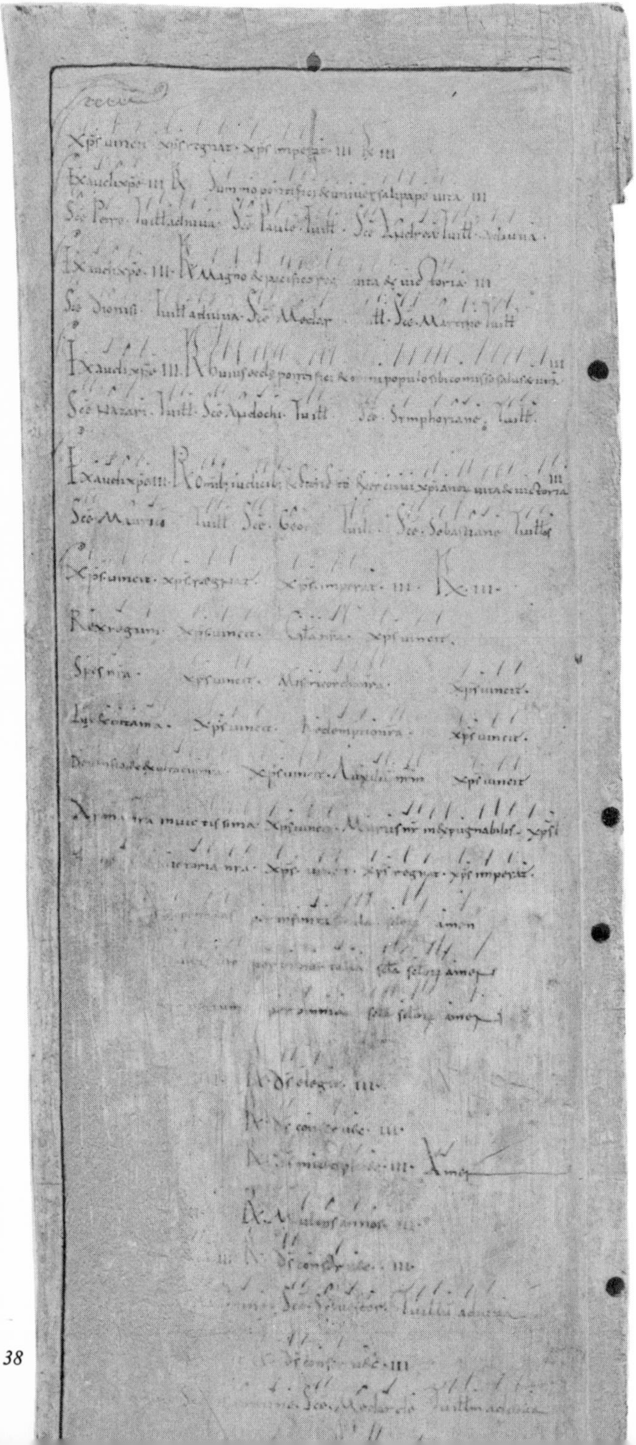

DOMINICA I DE ADVENTV D

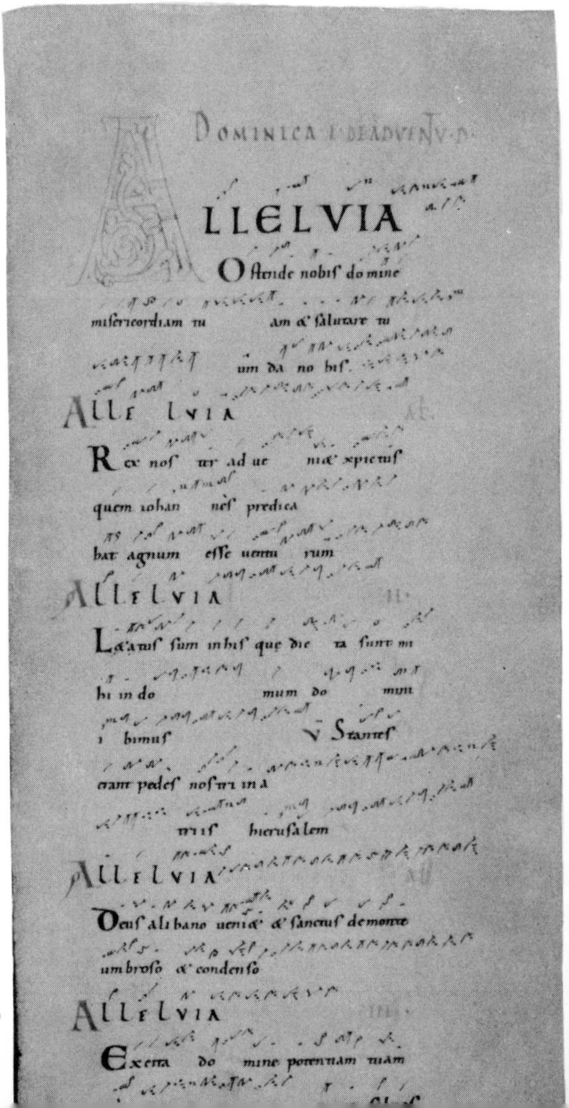

ALLELVIA

Ostende nobis domine
misericordiam tu   am et salutare tu
   um da no bis.

ALLELVIA

Rex nos ter ad ue   niae xpieus
quem iohan   nes predica
bat agnum esse uentu rum

ALLELVIA

Laetatus sum in his que dic ta sunt mi
hi in do   mum do   min
i bimus   Stantes
erant pedes nostri in a
    triis hierusalem

ALLELVIA

Deus ab ano ueniae et sanctus de monte
umbroso et condenso

ALLELVIA

Excita do mine potentiam tuam

38 Litanies written in neumes.
(diptych of the 9th and 10th centuries)
39 The Alleluia of the Munich Bible.
40 Extract from 9th century
manuscript, Vatican.
41 Musical notation of the 10th century.
Note that neither Byzantium nor
Rome retained the alphabetical
notation which was in use in
the Mediterranean region up to the
4th century. There was apparently
no notation in the West before
the 9th century, when a finished
system (neumes) appeared. Its
origins are obscure.

42 *Fragment of a manuscript from St. Gallen, 9th century, the "Glorification of Jesus," showing the twelve disciples.*
43 *Angel playing the trumpet. Manuscript from St. Gallen. In the 9th and 10th centuries, this Benedictine monastery was an important musical center.*

42

There was no pause in the amazing tempo of that musical and religious progress which was to endow the Church with liturgy inseparable from the very essence of Christianity.

There were musicians, however, who had an irresistible urge to create new ways of praising God, and they found it difficult to obey the rules laid down by St. Gregory and reinforced by Charlemagne's subsequent decree that those rules were to be observed. There was, therefore, a certain amount of subterfuge and evasion. After all, thought the musicians, even though we may not compose new pieces for the liturgy, what is there to prevent us from embroidering and developing the old forms in various ways? The sequence and the trope were devices of this nature, nothing more or less than a kind of safety valve or outlet for an initial burst of enthusiasm—they detracted nothing from it, but restrained and contained it. It needed nothing more than Notker's example to spark a veritable explosion of lyricism throughout the length and breadth of Christendom.

The movement began at Jumièges, near Rouen. St. Gall in Switzerland became its center. There was an important Benedictine monastery at St. Gall.

Some of the monks at Jumièges, trying to find a way to memorize the long vocalizations of the

44 The Apocalypse of St. John from Reichenau (ca. 1020). The monastery at Reichenau on Lake Constance resumed the tradition of St. Gall. It favored instrumental music (organ, harp, flute, trumpet, cymbals, cithara and three-string lyre).

45 David with his harp, musicians with long-handled cymbals, and, below them, dancers. (Psalter from St. Gall, ca. 850)

Alleluia in the Gradual, had hit upon the idea of fitting words to them. After the Normans had burned down their monastery, one of the monks sought shelter at St. Gall, taking the antiphonary with him. Notker the Stammerer (Balbulus) caught sight of the antiphonary and noticed the verses that had been added by the monks at Jumièges. Fascinated by the idea, he adopted it himself and by reason of his talent created a great reputation for it. Let us quote from a valuable work by Charles-Albert Cingria:[20]

"The Stammerer says that it was in order not to forget the tune that he invented the words, as a kind of memory exercise, and that he had copied the idea from someone else. One may possibly not believe him; if there had been no Notker, the preliminary, tentative efforts at Jumièges, or anywhere else for that matter, would not have developed as they did. More important still, the art of sequence writing would not have received from Pope Nicholas I (858-867) the approval which gave it the seal of legitimacy. If we assume, in the first place, that the real composer of *anything* is the man who regulates, adjusts and aligns it, it is possible to accept Notker's own words, that he was not the inventor, but the composer. For example, it is said that France was 'composed' by her kings; that the Code was 'composed' by Justinian. Be

that as it may, it was through Notker and from . . . St. Gall that the movement spread from place to place. There is another reason why Notker did not really consider himself the father of the sequence. He had read Virgil and knew what poetry was."

Notker was not at all sure, we are told, that "the well-arranged, harmonious words he wrote were in fact poetry, despite the pleasure they accorded him. He believed them to be more in the nature of prose." And so "proses" they were called. "The style spread like wildfire. Schools sprang up everywhere; it traveled from Switzerland into France, then to England and Germany, and even into Southern Italy. It caught on amid the snows of Norway and Sweden, too, for before very long, there were many collections of sequences and tropes in every corner of Europe."

Notker's own famous words are perhaps best quoted here: "Often, in my childhood, the long melodies which my fickle young heart had learned deserted me and I used to wonder what I could do to remember them. It was then that a monk from Jumièges appeared. He sought refuge, for his monastery had but lately been burned to the ground by the Normans. This monk had with him a manuscript wherein I observed certain words written into the melodic extensions of the Alleluia; but

46

they were full of mistakes. I was as loth to practice them as I was happy to have discovered them. I found it preferable to imitate the style in my own way, and I began to write *Laudes Deo concinat Orbis universus, Qui gratis est liberatus* and, further on, *Coluber Adae malesuasor.* When my master, Iso, had seen these pieces, he congratulated me on my work, though at the same time he regretted my lack of experience. He then praised those passages that had pleased him and took the trouble to rewrite those he had liked least, commenting: 'You have to make each single syllable correspond to the movement of the melody.' As a result of his words, I rewrote those passages that corresponded to *IA,* in order to make them flow more smoothly. Those that corresponded to *LE* or *LU* I left aside as being impossible to adapt, though later I was to find this easy, as can be seen from *Dominus in sina* and *Mater.* The idea took great hold of me, and I lost no time in dictating a second series, *Psallat Ecclesia mater inlibita.* When I presented these to master Marcellus, he was delighted; he assembled them on parchment and gave them to the children to sing. . . ."[21]

We should remember that these famous vocal exfoliations or *jubili* ("jubilation" has the same root as "yodel," whose meaning is obvious) often originated from popular little airs, which we might describe today as "catchy tunes." They were very much in fashion during the last years of the French Empire. They were hummed by everyone, in the fields, in the streets, on rivers as they pulled the boats along. "It was," says Cingria, "the new popular music, in Syrian style; and in the same way that we cannot prevent the importation of Anglo-Negro syncopation, it was likewise impossible, for any length of time, to restrain this art which had for so long been held in check by statesmen and philosophers, and people abandoned themselves to it wholesale. It lacked poetry, however, and it was Notker who marshalled the results of the first faltering experiments and found for the art a form of its own."

St. Augustine wrote that a jubilant man expresses his joy in wordless sound. His joy is too great for words; they are no longer adequate, and he abandons himself to a cry of sheer happiness where words have no place. Jubilation may be secular; it may be religious; it may even be licentious. "So that you may better understand what I wish to say," says Saint Augustine, "turn your minds to something with which you are quite familiar—that is, the jubilation of those who work on the land, who reap, and labor in the vineyards; remember the ceaseless and joyful song they sing, these people who are so overwhelmed by the

47

46 Group of musicians, with horn, and stringed instruments played by plucking. (Psalter from Stuttgart—9th century)
47 King David playing the harp. A musician with long-handled cymbals plays before the king. (Psalter from Stuttgart—9th century)

earth's fruitfulness that they begin to sing. They exult in words at first, and then, unable to contain themselves any longer, they burst forth into wordless song."

It is useful to have this definition of jubilus or vocalization before us, for we are thereby better able to grasp what happened at St. Gall. To quote Cingria once more—nobody understood more about it than he did—what happened was "a phenomenon something like that which Nietzsche describes when he says that initially Greek art had a musical (Dionysian) origin and was, properly speaking, anti-intellectual. In actual fact, the primary urge in all primitive poetry was never the subject, nor the ethics—though these had their uses—nor reason, nor emotion . . . the primary element was the chorus or refrain, which expressed not itself (for that would be art for art's sake), but the very essence of existence itself." These are wonderful words, which might very well sum up the entire history of music. For what, when all is said and done, is it all about? Is it the analysis of forms and the classification of facts, or is its real purpose the desire to understand why, since the dawn of creation, man has gone doggedly on singing and fashioning musical instruments?

"Notker," says the poet Ekkehard (who was born in 973 and who also lived at St. Gall), "in appearance was slight of stature; but only in body, not in spirit. He stammered when he spoke, but there was no such faltering in his soul. He was forever reaching out for things above himself; he bore his afflictions with exemplary patience. He was of gentle disposition, yet at the same time most punctilious in everything that had to do with monastic life. He was somewhat timid and shy, and when at any time he was in some respect caught unawares, he would fight most courageously against the evil spirits that assailed him. At prayer, at recitation, and when there was writing or composing to be done, there was none to compare with him."

Notker was born at Elgg, of noble family descended both from the Carolingians and the ancient Saxon kings. He is considered to be the greatest poet of the Middle Ages.[22]

There follows, by way of example, his Easter Sequence, pure and crystal clear in its simplicity:

La nature rend hommage au Sauveur ressuscité
    sorti de la nuit du tombeau.
Fleurs et champs ensemencé s'éveillent
    à la vie nouvelle;
Après la givre de l'hiver, le choeur des oiseaux
    se répand en hymnes de joie.
Et la lune et le soleil, que la mort du Christ avait
          obscurcis,

✝ HIC EST DAVID FILIVS · IESSE · TENENS

PSAL   TERIVM
INOMA   NIB: SVIS·
HEC   EST FORMA
PSAL   TERII·

DVO BVNIBVLA spe
AEGVALIA

✝ hec ē forma h
hoc BVNIBVL vo
FISTVLA   ser
hec   x
BV   la
cu   fis TVLi
medio pos
sed tria t

hec ē
eivs de

QVATTV
CORDAS habe
LIGNO medvl
CHORVS

48

48 King David playing a stringed instrument.
In the Middle Ages this Old Testament king
provided a popular theme. It was just as
popular as the theme of Orpheus and
his lute would become during the Renaissance.
(Bologna Library)
49 Psaltery with 10 strings. (Psalter from
Stuttgart—9th century)

49

brillent maintenant avec plus d'éclat.
Revêtue d'une verte parure, la terre célèbre
   le Ressucité,
Elle qu'un sourd tremblement ébranla
   le jour de sa mort.

          (*Analecta Hymnica, L III, 66*)[23]

"All Nature pays homage to the Risen Savior who came forth from the darkness of the tomb. The newborn flowers and new-sown fields awake unto new life; after winter frost the birds fill the heavens with a joyous chorus of song. And moon and sun, hidden in darkness as Christ died, shine brighter than ever. Clothed in her mantle of green, the earth gives praise to our Risen Lord, that earth which trembled in an earthquake on the day of His death."

We have already said that the sequences and prose hymns of Notker and the School of St. Gall spread with extraordinary rapidity and success. They were copied and imitated everywhere; variations of them developed in the different regions.

"It was like a sudden squall," says Cingria; and Chailley speaks in terms of "a frenzy."

After the Alleluia had been embroidered with melodic extensions and embellishments, attention turned to the *Kyrie,* where the final *E* was now in

its turn reinforced with words. As they developed, these proses acquired an independent character of their own, forming an entity in themselves. Once independent, they parted company with the main piece that had brought them into being and were performed by themselves. For instance, the *Ave Verum* became quite separate from the *Sanctus.* Later examples are the *Dies Irae* by Thomas Celano, a Franciscan, and the lovely *Stabat Mater* by Jacopone da Todi.

With Notker, Tutilo is the next best-known musician from St. Gall. He was a pupil of Iso and Marcellus about the year 900. While Notker distinguished himself principally in the art of sequence writing, Tutilo excelled at the trope, which was by then no longer a prolongation of a liturgical chant, but an addition to it, or a paraphrase of it, or sometimes, an interpolation into it.

The tradition of St. Gall was continued at a nearby monastery—the famous monastery at Reichenau on Lake Constance, by Hermannus Contractus, who was also the author of a valuable work on the musical concepts of his time. At St. Martial in France, too, "the gay, sublime sequence writers of Limoges"[24] kept up the tradition, as did Adam de St. Victor, whom Amédée Gastoué (writing around the turn of this century) called "the Notker of the 12th century."

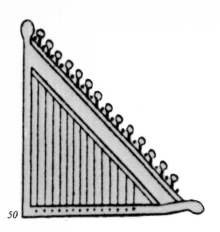

The importance of the sequence in relation to the ultimate development of Western music can be gauged by the fact that it was to give birth to the popular written song, as well as to the lyrics of the troubadours, and, finally, to the Christian theatre. "In Italy, too, the regular sequence is carrying all before it, with tender, mystical and secular compositions, and it is developing a form into which Dante need do no more than pour his inimitable genius."[25]

Music Outside the Church

During the first centuries of Christianity, some Church leaders wanted to ban all music from the services. Up to the 9th and 10th centuries they did manage to keep instruments outside the Church. Throughout the first thousand years, warnings against wandering minstrels were a regular feature.[26] These musicians were considered guilty of spreading and perpetuating pagan music. The very frequency of the warnings is an indication of the extent to which the Church had failed in its attempt to eliminate the desire people felt for this music, which came along to enhance the pleasures of their holidays and merrymaking. In vain did the Church seek to persuade the faithful that there was no surer instrument of the devil than the music of

minstrels and jongleurs, but there was nothing they could do; in some places, the people were even refused Holy Communion; even this was of no avail.

The clergy, it seems, were by no means unanimous in their disapproval.[27] In any case, as we shall see, the princes of the Church themselves were among the first to maintain instrumentalists among their entourage, just as much as the princes of the world.

St. Gall provides us with an excellent example of the way in which the monasteries had, with the passage of time, worn down the ecclesiastical disapproval of instruments. The facts are interesting. At its height, in the 10th and 11th centuries, the important Benedictine center at St. Gall sheltered a whole galaxy of singers, scribes, teachers and artists. It had a remarkable library, and it was also at the forefront of all the German monastic schools. On several occasions, royalty was welcomed to the monastery; there was Louis the German, Charles the Fat (839-888), Otto the Great (912-973), Henry III (1015-1066). The interesting fact is that they were welcomed, not merely with singing, but with ensembles of instruments, too.[28]

That devout monk of the 13th century, Johannes Ekkard, has something to tell us of the man Tutilo: "He was one of those men whom Flavius described when speaking of the way in which ath-

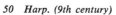

50 Harp. (9th century)
51 Central ornament, from a
Charles the Bald Bible.
52 Celtic crouth of the 9th century.

52

letes should be chosen—quick-moving and supple of limb. He was uncommonly skilled in the art of painting and carving the ivory plaques for book-binding; moreover, like his companions, he was also a musician. He was experienced in the use of wind instruments, for it was his habit to gather together the children of noble families, in a place which the Abbot appointed for the purpose, in order to teach them to play the flute. He could turn his hand skillfully to anything, no matter what, and could express himself in both languages. He could be serious or carefree as occasion demanded, so much so, that one of our kings, Charles le Gros, once cursed the fates which had decreed that such a man should be a monk."

This same Tutilo used to sing his tropes during the services to the accompaniment of a small lyre called a *fidicula*. "It is not too much to say," says Cingria, "that he, together with Iso and the Irish-man Marcellus, were still the same stock as the bards"—those bards whose epics Charlemagne used to make his scribes put in writing, and who were by no means extinct. We should remember that there were Druids in England up to the 5th century.[29] Chronicles have preserved the name of the blind epic poet Bernlef, a native of Frisia and "an expert in the art of reciting, to the accompaniment of the lyre which he played himself, stories of the ancients or of the battles of kings." Bernlef became a Christian in the 9th century.

We have now reached the point when the *Niebelungenlied* was appearing. "Barbarian" and Latin traditions finally merged. The Niebelungenlied were the German epics of the early 13th century, and they comprised numerous mythical poems or sagas. Wagner's "Der Ring des Niebelungen" was based largely on Norse legends and on the Niebelungenlied.

St. Gall gave us a typical work, in this connection, in the "Waltharius," long attributed to Ekkard. It is a gem of this revival of German poetry. In this work Virgilian ideas meet up with those of the old German songs.

Two worlds were moving into each other; one stretched northwards from the Mediterranean, the other moved down in the opposite direction. We should not have a true picture of these years of transition if we did not remember, too, the harsh—though not entirely unpolished—songs of Germany, as well as the shadowy figures of northern bards from Scandinavian regions. In his masterly work on the barbarian world, Gonzague de Reynold mentions both. "It is night. In the great round hall, with its painted and sculptured beams, a single pillar supporting the roof, the chief is installed upon a raised dais, surrounded by his followers.

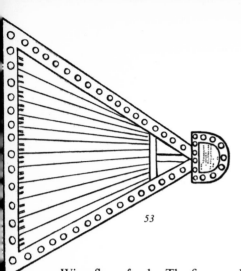

53

Wine flows freely. The fires are lit, and the flames dance upon the trophies hung upon the walls. The bard rises, a warrior among warriors. The song he sings is manly and rough, like something hewn out with a hatchet. The men around him are tired after their day's hunting or fighting, but they are beginning to relax now that they have eaten and drunk, and the feelings which the singer's voice arouses in them are swift, sharp and violent, like sword-thrusts or blows from a sledge-hammer. There is no halfway stage—the song is tightly coiled within itself, like a spring, as it were, ready to unwind. If the singer did not know how to keep his listeners breathless with anticipation, they would quickly tire and lose interest. So, from the very first word he dramatizes, adopting the very voices and gestures of his characters, bringing his scenes to life. Immediately, the listening warriors see their own lives reflected in these adventures; they see themselves in these heroes. They are quickly and completely won over by the passion and fire of the poet, and they become actors putting on their own show.

"These songs are neither primitive nor ordinary; centuries of tradition have gone into them. They are skillfully expressive and never imitative. They are rather like what the Germans call *Stabreim,* or alliterated verse, a clever style with a heavy, hammered-out rhythm which gives a powerful effect.

What practice the singer needed, to say nothing of a superb memory, to master his art! For here we are dealing with meter and verse which demanded great skill. Alas, for us, Charlemagne's collection has been lost, though we do still have the oldest poems of the 'Edda' [the name given to two collections of the legends and myths of old Scandinavian peoples]. However, when compared to the first 'Lieder,' they already show something of a modern streak."[30]

So much for the Germans.

For the Celts, bards came third in the hierarchy. They ranked next to the Druids and soothsayers. In Celtic society, especially in Ireland, order of rank was strictly observed. At the court of Tara, where the king lived, protocol was as rigidly observed as in any Eastern court, and disaster followed swiftly upon any breach of the rules or any inadvertent oversight of protocol.[31] The Gauls had their bards right up to the 8th century, and as late as the 12th century there were still some in England, at Cornwall. In Ireland, they lasted into the 17th century.[32]

We may seem to have strayed far from St. Gall and Lake Constance. Not at all. There were close links between St. Gall and the monks in Ireland. There is evidence of these links in the methods of illumination used on manuscripts. Dom Leclerq

52

53-54 Types of psalteries. We might mention here the symbolic performances which were often staged right up to the 18th century. "The psalter," said Cassiodorus in the 6th century, "is a most appropriate symbol of our Lord's body, for it is its upper tones that we hear as the body of Christ celebrates here below His glorious manifestations from above." (In Psalmis)

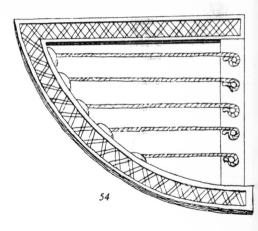

54

writes: "The relations which existed between St. Gall and Ireland are well known to us. For a long time there was an endless procession of Irish monks wending their way to this famous monastery. Its distant location, outside the shores of their native land, made it irresistibly alluring to this race of wanderers." [33] In 991 three monks at St. Gall were natives of Ireland.

It is impossible to exaggerate the importance of the cultural centers established by certain monasteries. There, far from the capital cities, in the boundless freedom of spiritual brotherhood, Europe was slowly and naturally finding its soul.

An interesting example of this sense of freedom in the monasteries is provided by an event that occurred in the year 829, and it concerns instrumental music at which the Church looked so askance. In that year, the monks at Reichenau appeared before Charles the Bald with an ensemble which comprised flutes and cymbals and an organ. "Most of us," we are told by one of the community there, "from our early years, had learned to sing or to play an instrument. One played the organ, which was the only instrument played in church. Another used to play the harp, yet another the flute or trumpet or trombone; some were experts on the triangular or three-string lyre. All of us, at one time or another, received instruction in the use of some particular instrument, and spent a great deal of our time practicing." [34]

We must not forget that we are still in the age of monody. The tune was taken care of by the organ, the wind instruments and the viols. The harps, played in rhythm, together with the cymbals and kettledrums, punctuated the melody as required. This is yet another example—virtually the last—of music that combined the differing sounds of both ancient and Oriental music.

At the beginning of the 12th century, a monk schooled in Platonic traditions, from Regensburg, was to build a symbolic organ, in which the psalter was likened to the soul (a sharp, high sound) and the cithara to the body (because of its lower sound). It will help, for an understanding of this symbolism, to recall that Plato, who died in 348 B.C., taught that the soul existed before birth, and that our search for knowledge is an effort by the soul to remember what the shock of birth caused it to forget. To be sure, the Regensburg monk was unaware that ancient India had had very similar ideas. (It is strange to see how music, down the ages, has been the vehicle for a certain number of ideas and symbols which crop up again and again, in various forms, regardless of the beliefs prevailing at the time.)

There was no dearth of clerics to condemn this

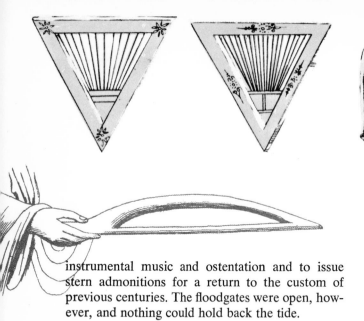

instrumental music and ostentation and to issue stern admonitions for a return to the custom of previous centuries. The floodgates were open, however, and nothing could hold back the tide.

Birth of a Christian Theatre

Greek tragedy grew out of the religious ritual pertaining to Dionysus, which was embedded in song and dance. Dionysus, often called Bacchus by both Greeks and Romans, was the god of wine. It was the trope, also both sacred and musical, that was to give birth to our theatre. In brief, the trope consisted of additional words supplied to the liturgical text. These words commented on the text and provided one syllable for each note of the melody, which had become extremely elaborate. Sometimes the tropes also supplied new melodies.

Gustave Cohen and Jacques Chailley have clearly demonstrated that our classical theatre is in no way a direct imitation of ancient drama, as was thought for a long time. It is more in the nature of a development of medieval liturgical drama. "Throughout the texts handed down to posterity from classical Antiquity, the idea of theatre had disappeared."[35] What happened under the Pharaohs in Egypt, in India, China and Japan, and in Athens, was to happen again—"because every re-

ligion," writes Cohen, "generates its own drama." The moment finally comes when some particularly popular or theatrical incident in the life of the god being celebrated takes on a visual aspect, in temple or church at first, with no renunciation of its sacred character.

Obviously, this is merely a brief outline of the process; scenery grew more complicated, non-religious elements gradually crept in, to such an extent that eventually it became necessary for the whole thing to be performed outside the temple or church, out of a sense of respect for holy places. Music began to play a diminishing role, and in societies where the framework of tradition was weak, its role disappeared completely in the end, and performances were entirely secular. There is no better proof than this sequence of events of the irrational, magic and, in the broadest sense of the term, religious quality of music.

Two particular events in the life of Christ, celebrated as Feast days by the Christian Church, invited this kind of dramatic development: the Nativity, a feast of joy, and Easter, the drama of death and Resurrection.

The first text to mention a liturgical drama dates from the 10th century (970). It gives very precise details of how it was performed. We are indebted for this to St. Ethelwold, who sent it to the monks

55

56   57   58   59

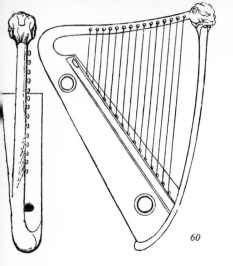

60

at Winchester, mentioning the fact that he had borrowed the idea from a church on the banks of the Loire:

"While the Third Lesson is being sung, a monk with a palm in his hand should approach the tomb. At the singing of the Third Response, three other monks come in, and also approach the tomb, picking their way carefully, as if looking for something. This represents the angel seated at the tomb and the three women bearing spices to anoint Christ's body. When the monk who is seated at the tomb sees the others, he should begin to sing softly and gently: 'Quem quaeretis?' (Whom seek ye?). And when he reaches the end, the three reply in chorus, 'Jesum Nazarenum' (Jesus of Nazareth)." This performance was based on a trope on the Pascal Introit *Resurrexi* by Tutilo.

The first step was now taken.

The church to which St. Ethelwold referred was the Abbey of Fleury-sur-Loire, now St. Benoit-sur-Loire, which together with St. Martial at Limoges was one of the centers of Latin drama. G. Cohen called it "the metropolis of liturgical drama." There they had a considerable repertory of plays on the resurrection, Christmas, the Massacre of the Innocents and the Miracles of St. Nicholas.

From the end of the 11th century, on each Christmas Day, the *Drama of the Nine Prophets* was presented. One after another, summoned by the choir, there appeared the nine Hebrew prophets who foretold the coming of Christ, and there were parts, too, for St. Elizabeth, for Nebuchadnezzar, and for the Sibyl and Virgil. The inclusion of this Latin poet is explained by his mysterious allusion to the birth of a child who, according to the promises of the Sibyl of Cumae, would put an end to the Iron Race and usher in a new golden age. In addition to these thirteen characters, there was the leading singer, whose job it was to introduce the Prophets. He would question them each in turn: "And you, what have you to tell us of Christ? Speak, for we listen!" Each character replied.

"There shall come forth a shoot from the stump of Jesse and a branch shall grow out of his roots, and the spirit of the Lord shall rest upon him," says the Prophet Isaiah (Isaiah XI:1-2). And John the Baptist, when questioned, replies: "I am not worthy even to untie the thong of His sandal." At the end of the play, the precentor concluded: "Oh ye disbelieving Jews, why do you still refuse to honor Christ?" The language used was Latin, and the whole thing, we repeat, was sung. Later there were novel extensions and picturesque innovations in staging. For instance, Balaam would appear on a real ass, with an "extra" hidden between the animal's feet, to speak the necessary words.[36]

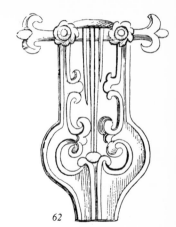

62

Among early liturgical plays, a special place must be given to *Sponsus* (The Spouse), where the theme is taken from the parable of the Wise and Foolish Virgins. It is a real little comedy, played and sung quite independently of any religious service. At the end, the Foolish Virgins were cast into Hell by a host of devils. This Hell was one of those great "jaws of Hell" in the head of a gaping monster, like those which appeared later in miracle and mystery plays. The devils set up a frightful din (whence the expression "a devil of a noise").[37]

Until quite recently, these early liturgical plays were studied from a purely historical point of view. Considerable credit is due to Chailley and Cohen, who promoted a theatrical company of students at the Sorbonne called the "Theophilians," for the successful and accurate reconstruction of these works, for it was a testimony of their remarkable artistic and dramatic value. The *Sponsus* was staged in 1934 at the Abbey of Fontgombaud, with the participation of the clergy and seminarists there. The results were most convincing.

Efforts were to culminate, in the 12th century, with the famous *Adam and Eve,* one of the first literary gems of the Middle Ages. This belongs as much to music as it does to literature, however, because of the supremely important part which music played in it, though this aspect was for a long time completely ignored by students of literature. Again, apart from a commentary spoken in dialogue verse, the *Adam and Eve* was entirely sung. It consisted of three parts. The first part is set in the Garden of Eden, where Adam and Eve, clad in white tunics, are set upon by an army of demons, gesticulating and grimacing, who proceed to tempt this first human pair to taste the Forbidden Fruit. After the pair's pitiful fall from grace, the devils cast them into the "mouth of Hell," which has been described elsewhere.

The second part tells the story of Cain and Abel.

The third part is the traditional *Drama of the Nine Prophets.*

With this work, plays left the church setting altogether, and from then on they were performed and sung on a platform set up on the open space in front of the church. The way was now open for mystery and miracle plays.

Latin was the chief language of all these plays, but the language of the people was also used in choruses sung by those who were present.[39] The music was frequently something of a mixture and, according to Chailley, "reflected the styles of the ages through which it had been composed and added to, rather like those churches that were begun in the Roman style and finished in flamboyant Gothic."

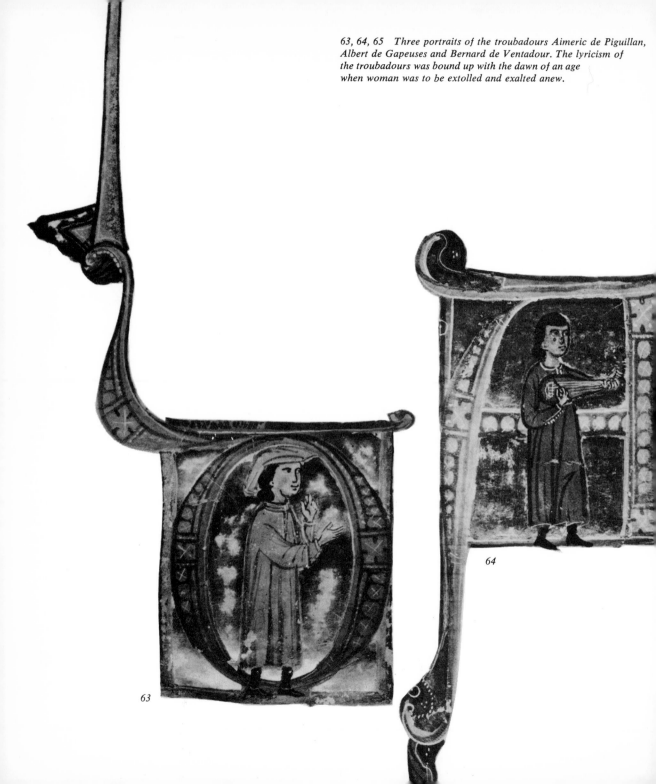

63, 64, 65 *Three portraits of the troubadours Aimeric de Piguillan, Albert de Gapeuses and Bernard de Ventadour. The lyricism of the troubadours was bound up with the dawn of an age when woman was to be extolled and exalted anew.*

63

64

Liturgical drama, then, sprang from the art of sequence and trope. It was this same art that was to create, from the end of the 9th century, an outburst of lyricism from the troubadours. The movement started in Aquitaine, not in Provence, as is often believed. It is worthwhile mentioning here that Aquitaine took in the Limoges area and thus included the Abbey of St. Martial, one of the French centers of sequence composition.

It has been said that the 12th century discovered love. The music of the troubadours was closely connected with this discovery, this dawn of new glory and new dignity for womanhood. All through the ages, it is true, poets have sung of the hopes and fears of lovers; of the sweet and wonderful charms of the beloved. The new element, in the lyricism of the troubadours, was that woman was placed on a pedestal, making her a great lady "with sovereign rights in matters of the heart."[40] The beloved was now free to hear the prayer of the suppliant lover or to reject it, as she chose. "Oh that it should please my lady to love me!" sighed Guillaume of Poitiers. The idea of "the joy of love" was something unknown to the ancient world or to Christianity before the 12th century. It has been defined as "an upsurge of emotion, where desire, though recognized, becomes transcendently spiritual, raising the beloved out of the ordinary world."

65

66   Folquet the troubadour who became
Bishop of Toulouse. The troubadours
composed their own songs. According
to their rank and fortune, they
would have at their service one
or more jongleurs who would play
and interpret their works.
(French 13th century manuscript)
67   Page from a Missal (ca. 1200).
It is written in neumes.
68   Musicians with harps and viols.
(13th century psalter)

(J. Belperron, *The Joy of Love,* 1948.) Guillaume of Poitiers explained it in the following words: "Man has never been able to grasp the nature of this joy, either through his will, his desire, his mind or his imagination. There is nothing to equal it, and the man who would praise it worthily would not be able to do so were he to try forever."

By supreme refinement, the joy may even be obtained when love is denied. Says Bernard de Ventadour: "My love for her is, however, so perfect that I weep; for me sighs are sweeter than satisfaction and joy. This love fills my whole heart with such fragrance that a thousand times a day I die of grief, to be born anew in happiness . . . this is such sweet sorrow, worth all in all to me."

All historians who have written about the troubadours have been struck by the same fact—although this poetry etherealized and exalted woman, it was not, however, based on vague and formless platonism. This contradiction led René Nelli to say that the troubadours compared woman "to that which they thought most pure, most unearthly, the most far removed from their fighting, heroic ego; and this at a time when they were giving play to their most warlike instincts." They worshiped woman to the point where they "raised her to a heaven from which her inaccessible love rains gently down as an undeserved favor."

What was the real meaning of courtly love? The question always raises controversy. Was it a quest for something, akin to the search for the Holy Grail in the series of romantic tales of King Arthur circulating at the same time? Or was it in the nature of a spiritual discipline? "Courtesy," wrote Belperron, "was the concern of men, in which woman played but an instrumental part." We know that in a remarkable essay Denis de Rougemont inclined to the view that the lyricism of the troubadours was of Albigensian origin. This heresy had taken its name from the town of Albi in Provence. We can no more deny the possible influence of that heresy, rampant at the time in southern France, than we can that of the Arabian poetry which was then flourishing in Spain. Whatever its origin, whether French, Albigensian or Arabian, each theory has produced many brilliant and serious works.

It is worthwhile, in addition, to dissociate the ideological content of this lyricism from its musical support. Although the former might well have been inspired by an influx of Eastern or gnostic ideas, perhaps through the spread of heresy or through Arabian poetry and mysticism, the origin of the music is no longer in doubt, thanks to the clear and lucid exposition of Jacques Chailley, who is one of the greatest living authorities on medieval music.

nas mar nõ mou
souen. Que ieu p̃
nas del rey auslire.
ar march fuit enar
mescl amen. Er enaiſ
toblar men on marai
Jas mier morir nos
hom eſcrurit. El ſer
is es mi mil ans pl
los. Que tebe mill auira te ra guizardos.

P er quer pecatz amois ſo ſabetz uos. Si
uſhes ips nas uoſnom adue. Que nop ſe
rs reu dan mainras faſes. Que ſon amic
peir om ſo aug due. Queus aiſtenir er a
car nomen uire. Gan ſaber quen guied
ngnen. Ai poder uos el ſcuici eſſamen.

O uos dõ fia que auetz mandamen. fox
e amor eues au rm deſire. Nõ grey m
p diech chauſmen. Gan rm gn uos p̃
mer ioſine. Quel car plora em uoſe

Dom̄ pm̄a ī aduentu dñi.

A te leuaui animam meam de[us]

us meus in te cōfi do non eru

bescam neq; irrideant me mi

nimici mei et enim uniuer si qui

te expectant n̄ cōfundentur

Vias tuas domine notas fac michi et semitas tuas edoce me.

Pf'a euouae gl Vniuer si qbu te expectant non cō[n]

fundentur dōmine V Vias tuas domine

notas fac mic hi et se mitas tu[as]

as edoce me Al' uia V Osten

69 Detail from a tapestry from
the Cathedral at Gerona, Spain.
The full tapestry depicts Christ
as God of all the Universe.
At each corner naked children,
seated on deflating goatskin bottles,
typify the wind as they blow on
double horns. This detail shows
one of the corners.

Etymology tells us that "troubadour" is in fact "trobador" or "finder," a musician with an aptitude for "inventing" words and music. But the word "trobador" was originally the "tropator" or "maker of tropes." Chailley concedes that this trace-back in etymology is quite feasible. Indeed, it seems less forced than that put forward by the Spanish musicologist Ribera. According to that scholar, "troubadour" appears to derive from the Arabic noun *tarab* meaning "music" and from the Romance ending *dour*, whence we get *tarabour*, which would mean merely a "player of music," not a composer. *Montrib,* another Arabic word, from the same root, would seem to have a similar meaning.[41]

In Limoges, at the Abbey of St. Martial, the trope had undergone overall changes, and as a result it gradually lost all connection with the piece it was supposed to begin or end. It was now independent, and was inserted between two points of the liturgy. We shall see how it led, later, to the *conductus* or "lead-song," to which we shall refer again when dealing with the origins of polyphony. What we are concerned with here is how this independent trope engendered a whole repertory of pieces which were used to fill in the "blank" moments of the service.

They were at first called *versus* (verses). Then they were called "composition in verse." Sometimes they were even written with the words in the vernacular. Now the first troubadours, who came from the same region—Limoges—also called their songs "verses" at first. Guillaume de Poitiers wrote: "I want it to be known that it is of good quality, this little verse from my workshop; it is a fact that in this kind of work I offer only the choicest, and when I release this verse I shall point to it as proof of that."

Chailley's theory (which was supported in Germany by Hans Spanke) relates these verses from the first troubadours to the Latin *versus* from the Abbey of St. Martial, which had themselves sprung from the trope. "In this way, the origins of liturgical plays, epic poetry, lyric poetry, and to some extent, polyphony, are joined in one coherent cycle."[42] This is the most logical of the many conflicting theories that exist; and it has the advantage of leaving the door open for a variety of interpretations as far as idealistic influences are concerned, while establishing quite firmly the music's origin.

It would be wrong, moreover, to isolate the lyricism of the troubadours from the atmosphere of great general stimulation prevailing in those early days of the second thousand years of Christianity. The long period of darkness that followed the fall of the Empire, the intermingling of different races and tongues, the incessant clash of violence

70

and the impact of new settlements produced what Cohen has called "the splendor and light of the Middle Ages." All over the West, cathedrals were springing up; there was feverish building everywhere. South of the Loire, romance art was in full flower. Already, as the 12th century dawned, there was a great surge of adoration which inspired men to build higher and still higher into the heavens. Pillars and arches grew loftier, while walls grew less bulky, transformed into great windows with stained glass. Gothic was making its appearance on the Ile de France. Devotion to the Blessed Virgin was developing with astonishing fervor, as if in response, in some mystical way, to the exaltation of woman by poets and writers. Men of letters had taken to translating Ovid and his *Art of Love* in preference to Virgil.

In southern France, the Albigensian heresy was assuming proportions that alarmed the Church. In Italy, St. Francis of Assisi, Il Poverello, unleashed a great movement for a return to conscious emotions, and his love of humble things, of plants and of beasts, was to transform the very vision of painters themselves. They took to looking at reality with new eyes and new hearts and were preparing to apply their skills from an entirely new approach.

In northern France, we find a society with considerable liberty of manners and customs and with considerable freedom of thought. Rich, powerful men, like the Duke of Aquitaine or the Count of Toulouse, were carefully guarding their independence from the King, who had practically no means of enforcing his authority, at any rate over these feudal barons of the south. As for the Church, it was vigorous and well disciplined in the north, but, south of the Loire, there is room to believe that it had, in general, "opted out."[43] Priests were no longer celibate. "The most important of the clergy live in the manner of Lords. The aristocracy maintains vast estates, keeping up lesser courts in their castles." Orderic Vital (13th century) tells us: "There is a fashion for enormous sleeves, falling over the hands, and shoes with stuffed toes, making them look like scorpions' tails." And Geoffrey de Vigeois, a little later, remarks: "People have taken to making rich and costly materials, with colors to suit all moods; hems are adorned by having little circles cut out of them, or are cut in points, making their wearers look rather like the devils which painters portray. Young people are wearing their hair long, and their shoes have long tongues. So voluminous are the garments, that the women look like grass snakes as they trail their gowns behind them."

70 *Alfonso X of Spain, called The Wise (1252-1284). His court was an important musical center. He was the author of a number of "Canticles of Saint Mary" (musical poems dedicated to the Blessed Virgin).*
71 *Richard Lionheart, King of England. His mother, Eleanor of Aquitaine, gave him a love of poetry. His name has remained associated with the lyricism of the trouvères.*

71

It was in such a society, whose habits were a source of amazement to northern France—a society, it seems, ready for all and any adventure of body or soul—that the troubadours were to develop, to live, to love, to write and to compose.

The first troubadour about whom anything is known was William IX, Count of Poitiers and Duke of Aquitaine (1071-1127). His estates were virtually a kingdom in themselves, and he was absolute master. He took part in the First Crusade, without much conviction, it seems. When he returned, it was not an epic or chivalrous poem he composed, but a droll poem about his own adventures, which "he used to recite joyfully, before princes and great men." (Vital). His relations with the Church were openly hostile. He never missed an opportunity to seize Church possessions, though this in no way prevented him, when he felt his immortal soul might be in danger, from making the pilgrimage to Compostella, the shrine of St. James, in Spain. De Vigeois states, "He was mad about women," and he was accused of having built an abbey which was full of prostitutes. Yet this playboy was to write: "My destiny has always been such that no joy ever came to me from what I loved. It was always thus and always will be so, for at the moment of fulfillment my heart would whisper: 'All, all is vanity'."

There is one item of interest that concerns William IX. He had married the widow of King Sancho-Ramiro of Aragon and used to make frequent visits to Spain, where his two brothers-in-law lived. On the whole, relations between Christians and Moslems were excellent, especially in aristocratic circles. Young nobles would spend some time in Moslem courts to receive training for knighthood, for the Moors were regarded both as knights and as noblemen.[44]

Moreover, if there is any substance in the idea that the inhabitants of southern France—Provençals, to distinguish themselves from the French in the north—felt more in common with their Spanish neighbors than with their northern countrymen, then the "arabization" theory is plausible.

The lyricism of the troubadours did not immediately achieve that subtle refinement which led to the idea of courtly love. From the first known pieces of William IX, to the poetic achievements of the *trobar ric* (rich trope), in which Arnaut Daniel and Raimbaut d'Orange excelled, to the almost esoteric refinement of the *trobar clus* (select trope), there was an interval of some years. In reference to the trobar clus, we should mention the names of Bernart Marti, Peire d'Auvergne and Guiraut de Borneilles. This interval, 1100 to 1282, was as long as that which elapsed between the first

72   73

performance of *Athalie* and the publication of *Les Miserables*.[45] The year 1282, incidentally, gave us a piece from Guiraut Riquier, one of the last troubadours worthy of the name.

Although one can detect the kernel of the idea of courtly love in William's songs, this lordly poet also left behind him convivial pieces on subjects later used by Boccaccio (1313–1375). These pieces were undoubtedly much bandied about in castles everywhere. They were frequently couched in the coarsest of language; but then, the people of the Middle Ages were no more afraid of life's realities than people at the time of the Renaissance. As yet, the moral climate was not of the kind that would give rise to the complexes which assail and torment "moralistic" societies.

The following story is the theme of one of William's songs:[46] Having left Auvergne one day, he meets the wives of Lord Garin and Lord Bernard. He replies to their friendly greetings with mere gibberish, so they conclude that he is deaf and dumb, and therefore, of a necessity, discreet. Thinking themselves in luck, they take him home with them, warm him up by a good fire, and give him food and drink. However, one of the women is overcome by last-minute doubts. Suppose he is not really deaf and dumb? They have to be sure. They undress him, then they go off to fetch a nasty

ginger cat. They put the animal on his shoulders, and then, tugging it by the tail, its claws all out, they pull it down the length of his back. He is stoic and there is not a squeak out of him. "He really *is* deaf and dumb," say the ladies. "Let's get the bath ready. Imagine the fun we will have!" The concluding words of the tale leave the imagination ample scope as to the nature of the fun.

During his lifetime, William had inculcated in his granddaughter, Eleanor, his own love of poetry. After his death, Eleanor would marry two kings: Louis VII and Henry Plantagenet (by whom she became mother of Richard Lionheart). But prior to these marriages, she gathered around her at Toulouse a court where troubadours and minstrels were always welcome. Of course, not all troubadours were men of noble birth, like William. Many of them, from humbler backgrounds, were, or had been, wandering minstrels. "The profession of the jongleur was invented by men of intelligence endowed with a certain amount of knowledge, to divert and honor nobility by the playing of instruments." This definition can be found in a letter from the troubadour Riquier to the King of Castile (1274). We shall return later to the role of the minstrel in medieval society and to that great brotherhood of instrumentalists and wandering comedians to which they belonged. Although a prince

72-73 *Bellringers of
the Middle Ages.*
74 *King David playing the harp.
(French-Flemish School—12th century)*

74

75

75   *Previous page:*
Harp-type psalteries.
76   *Previous page:*
Bagpipes, widely used in
the Middle Ages. They were
relegated to the world of
folk music after the
18th century.
77   *Psalteries from the*
psalter "Canticles of St. Mary."
(Manuscript from Escurial— 13th century)

like William could quite well be a troubadour and sing his songs himself, it would hardly be right to call him a jongleur. Troubadours composed. When fortune permitted, they had at their disposal one or more musicians who interpreted their songs for them and spread them around.

It is to Marcabru that we owe the trobar clus, the art of "mixing words together so as to give several possible meanings to the sentence, or even to make it no longer comprehensible at all."[47] Marcabru was never happy in love:

> *Marcabru, son of Marcabrune,*
> *Born under such fated stars*
> *That all he knows of love*
> *Is how it may deceive!*
> *Oh listen while I tell!*
> *For never did he fall in love,*
> *Or anyone love him.*

This esoteric art was followed by the trobar ric, characterized by its richness of style. The master of this shapely art, with its beautiful rhythm and clever rhyme, was Arnaut Daniel (1180-1210), whom Dante considered "a great craftsman."

Then there was Jaufré Rudel (1130-1150). He was the poet of "love from afar," that is, love that was not only unattainable, but unreal and spiritual-

73

78 Previous page: Lutes. This is a very ancient instrument and came to Europe in the 10th century. It was a stringed instrument which was plucked and played without a plectron. It had many forms.
79 Previous page: Viols.
80, 81, 82 Pythagoras and Phylolaüs working out note scales. (Wood carving, 15th century)

ized. "Let no one be surprised that I should love that which I can never attain, for my heart rejoices only in such love as this. For me there is no joy like unto this, and I know not what good it may bring to me." Or again: "I know full well that I have never possessed her; that she will never possess me. She will not count me her friend, nor make me any promise; I hear neither truth nor falsehood from her lips, and I know not if I ever shall."

This theme of love unattainable appears to have been borrowed from Arabian poetry.

Building on the verse of this Jaufré Rudel, a "biographer" of the Middle Ages thought up a story as charming and touching as it was legendary. The story was the inspiration for Rostand's *Distant Princess*. In the 14th century Petrarch used it, and so did Swinburne in the late 19th century. It is so characteristic of the spirit which animated the lyricism of the troubadours that it must be accorded a place here.

"Jaufré Rudel was of high birth, a prince of Blaye, who fell in love with the Countess of Tripoli. Although he had never seen her, he had heard many lovely things about her from pilgrims returning from Antioch. He wrote a great deal of poetry about her, with beautiful tunes, though his words were poor. Wanting to see her, he joined a crusade and set sail. He fell ill on the voyage and was put off at an inn in Tripoli. The Countess was told about it, and came to his bedside, where she took him in her arms. He recognized her, whereupon he praised God that he had been allowed to live until that moment. Then he died, in her arms. She had him buried with great honor in the house of the Templars. The very same day, she took the veil, because of the grief his death caused her."

It is in the work of Bernard de Ventadour that the idea of courtly love becomes crystallized, although Bernard was not the inventor of it. He is a good example of the *trobar leu* (free poetry), which is, as it were, the standard pattern.[48] Bernard sang only of love, without which life would be a living death.

"Dead indeed is he who does not feel in his heart the sweetness of love. What is life without love? Does not one become merely a trial to one's fellows? Please God that should I ever join the ranks of those who have never felt the desire for love, He will not hate me enough to let me breathe one single moment longer."

This love was less unreal than that of Jaufré Rudel:

"Alas! What good is my life, if I am never to see my one and only joy in all her beauty; to behold her body white as Christmas snow, so that we may know if in all things we are truly one."[49]

81

82

Bertrand de Born (1140–1215) was a warrior-poet from Périgord. Folquet, from Marseille, ended up wearing a bishop's mitre. Both were among a number of those who brought honor to the lyricism of southern France.

The Trouvères

The *trouvères* were the singers who used the language of northern France. The lyricism of the troubadours was so impregnated with the spirit of the sun-drenched south that one would have thought it well nigh incapable of spreading northwards. Yet it did, creating north of the Loire a "swift, over-riding fashion which wriggled its way in 'as Janroy tells us,' via those myriad secret ways which fashions always seem to find and which even the keenest historical investigations fail to uncover."[50] Not only did it become firmly established there, taking on a new lease of life, but its ideal of courtesy left a lasting mark on the community.

The art of the troubadours had found eloquent and persuasive advocates in the persons of the proud, high-spirited Eleanor of Aquitaine and her two daughters by Louis VII: Marie, Countess of Champagne, and Aelis, Countess of Blois. Marie of Champagne was able to attract to her court at Troyes writers like Chrétien, French poet and author of such chivalrous works as *Perceval* and *Lancelot*. It was no doubt Marie of Champagne who suggested to that writer the idea of putting the best from the troubadours into the language of the north.[51]

We shall find, as we did in southern France, many nobles and minstrels among the numerous trouvères. Among the former, the most outstanding were Thibaut IV, Count of Champagne and King of Navarre, as powerful a lord as William IX had been in Aquitaine, and Richard Lionheart of England. Eleanor of Aquitaine had appointed Richard, who was her son, as the administrator of her estates in Aquitaine, and it was there that he acquired a taste for poetry and adventure. All the same, for his songs he used the language of the north.

Richard's name in history is inseparable from that of his faithful minstrel, Blondel de Nesles, himself a first-class trouvère. When Richard was taken prisoner on his return from the Third Crusade, Blondel, says the legend, went off to join him in the Danubian fortress where he was held, and managed to secure his master's release by means of his singing.

Other trouvères and troubadours whose names we know are worthy of mention. Gautier d'Epinal, Conon de Béthume, Guiot de Provins, Gautier

77

d'Argies, and a lesser noble from Chartres, Colin Muset.

Troubadours and trouvères alike accompanied their songs with instruments, or to be more accurate, had them accompanied by a jongleur or minstrel. The instrument usually chosen was the vielle or viol, forerunner of the violin. It had three or four strings at first and later, in the 15th century, five strings, and could be tuned as required. It gave a very sweet sound and was played with a bow.

Those troubadour songs that time has preserved are written in the square notation which followed neumatic notation. The hooks, curves and dots that had appeared on the line notation (evolved by about the year 1000) were replaced with square notes, and dots were now a prominent feature. "A sign that in neumatic notation had indicated three, four or five sounds automatically became three, four or five *dots* placed on the lines and in the spaces."[52] There were no bars in this notation, and for a long time it was uncertain how these tunes should be read, as we do not know what the rhythm was. According to theories now generally accepted, the rhythm was based on the verse.

There was great variety in the forms used by both troubadours and trouvères. We have already said that the songs which preceded the songs of courtly love were flippant and suggestive. The crusade song was the *planhs,* or lament, a serious song which told of the death of a great one or a friend; it was a song of real life, which was to develop into a kind of satirical song, the *sirventès.* It would be quite natural to suppose that we are indebted to folk music for the pastoral and the shepherd-song. This is not so; in fact, these were inspired by the troubadours, and folk music took up the theme. Then there was the *canso,* or love song; also the *tenson,* which took the form of a rhymed dissertation usually, but not always, on the subject of love. There were also the "songs of daybreak," wherein a faithful friend kept watch to warn the lovers of the coming of the day.

There were two other styles: "Cours d'Amour" (Courses of Love) and "Puys d'Amour," its replica in the south. But these were ultimately reduced to utter absurdity by their own ridiculous affectation.

The Laudi

Although there were troubadours in Italy (Lanfranc, Abbot of Caen, Cigala of Genoa, Sordello of Mantua, Bartelommeo Zorsi, to name a few), it is not really to their works that we should look for the true heritage of southern lyricism. We should, rather, go to Petrarch and Dante. They regarded Arnaut Daniel, in particular, as the most important of the troubadours. It was Arnaut Daniel, whom we have mentioned already, that Dante had in mind when, in *De Vulgari Eloquentiae,* he referred to his use of the vernacular. "Hell, Purgatory and Paradise," writes Charles-Albert Cingria, "are one long poem with an underlayer of plainchant; it is a sequence in three parts."

Petrarch had been able to observe the troubadours at closer quarters than Dante, because of his sojourns in Provence. Both the Italian schools of poetry can be said to owe a great deal to the troubadours. The Sicilian school was much influenced by the genial Frederick II (1194-1250) and his court, though it remained cloistered, as it were, in barren imitation. More important, the Florentine school, with the creation of the *dolce stile nuovo* (sweet new style), also drew much of its inspiration from the troubadours. Both Petrarch and Dante went back to Arnaut Daniel for the sestina, from which they later produced the double sestina. The sestina has six stanzas, each of six lines.

More important still, however, for the history of music, was the parallel development in Italy of a new religious poetry, which found expression in the *laudi spirituali.* These were the inspiration of St. Francis of Assisi, who was exhorting his follower, the Friars Minor, to preach not only with

83 *The devil playing the viol. (Sculpture from Amiens Cathedral— 13th century)*

83

*84 Demon playing the horn.
(From a mural painting,
Trier Cathedral)*

words but with song. They were to become jong-leurs—"God's minstrels." As a result, there blossomed a new type of popular hymnody, which was utterly different from the clever art of the troubadours, even though there was a common origin, the sequence. "At St. Gall, as well as in other places, litanies, acclamations, tropes of the Gloria, are called laudi, and sequences also are sometimes so called."[53] If San Germano is to be believed, the crowds assembled by the followers of St. Francis heard first a trumpet, played by a friar *(Cum cornu quodam convocabit populum)* and then three Alleluias sung very loudly by the same friar. This could not have been anything except a Gregorian Alleluia. The people used to take up the refrain, adding the following tropes:

> *Benedictu laudatu et glorificatu lu Patre,*
> *Benedictu laudatu et glorificatu lu Filiu*
> *Benedictu landatu et glorificatu lu Spiritu*
> *Sanctu*
>
> *Alleluia, gloriosa Donna.*[54]

Gradually there came into being a whole repertory of religious songs, which a century later were to be the main influence on the Ars Nova (New Art). These hymns were not sung in church, but at meetings and processions. The singers who sang them were called *Laudisti* or *Laudesi* and were grouped into confraternities under the direction of a *capitani* (leader).

Spain and Portugal

While southern France was being laid waste by fire and sword during the unfortunate crusade against the Albigensians at the end of the 12th century, many troubadours sought refuge at the Court of Ferdinand II of Castile and at the courts of Catalonia. This crusade was led by Simon de Montfort; he was thorough, and he did a great deal toward destroying the high culture of the troubadours. In addition, barons of northern France, under pious pretexts, saw the crusade as a heaven-sent opportunity to seize lands that did not belong to them.

In Spain, however, the music of the troubadours went on. One of the Castilian kings, Alfonso II, was competing with the troubadours himself, for he had formed a friendship with Peire Vidal, a rather reckless and scatterbrained troubadour from Toulouse. One hundred years later, Alfonso X of Castile, known as Alfonso the Wise (1221-1284), made his court an important musical center, and history, literature and science are no less indebted to him than music. Serious study, culture and an inquiring mind had imbued Alfonso X with the greatest degree of tolerance, and at his court, musician and scholar could rub shoulders regardless of race or creed. Alfonso the Wise produced a number of scholarly works, and he had others translated from Arabic. These ranged from dissertations on navigation to discussions on chess, from philosophy to music and history, and in addition, he found time to compose almost 450 musical poems—the Canticles of the Holy Mary.

The canticle practiced at the court of Alfonso the Wise closely resembled the Marian hymns of Gautier de Coincy. The word "canticle" means a hymn or religious song. Like the Franciscan laudi and the French ballads (the virelai), the verse is preceded and followed by a refrain.

The manuscripts on which these royal canticles were written, at least those which have survived, are lavishly decorated and show the great variety of instruments in use in Spain at the time. There were more than thirty: the Moorish guitar (from the Greek kithara), brought in by the Arabs; the viol; the lute, one of the oldest instruments in the world; the double flute; and a number of others.[55]

The influence of troubadour music was active also in Portugal. There the *barcarolle,* or boat-song, was added to the various other styles that had been developed in France.

85-86 Minnesingers and knight. In German, "Minne" is "courtly love." The art of the Minnesingers is a faithful reflection of the joys and occupations of the knight—the love he shows his lady, the life he leads as a warrior, the tournament, the hunt. (14th century manuscript—Heidelberg Library) Figures 89 through 96 are from the same source.

The Minnesingers

The Minnesingers

The influence of southern music and poetry did not remain confined to the Latin countries; again, the impetus came from the upper stratum of society.

Frederick Barbarossa (*ca.*1125-1190), King of Germany and Emperor of the West from 1155, took as his second wife Beatrice of Burgundy. The trouvère Guiot de Provins was a member of her retinue. There was also the fact that French jongleurs traveled around a good deal and often wandered into foreign parts. It was by way of two currents—through the wandering musicians and through chivalry—that troubadour music spread from France to Burgundy, then to Switzerland and the German courts. Sometimes, however, the two currents were one and the same, for when great personages moved from place to place they took their musicians with them. It is no surprise to find that when Barbarossa went to France he had in his entourage one of the first Minnesingers, Friedrich von Husen. At first these singers adhered strictly to the pattern of the French school.

Courtly love became, in German, *Die Minne,* and the *Minnedienst* was the homage of love rendered to the lady.

Nevertheless, although the lyricism of the Minnesingers owed most of its themes to the courtly art of the troubadours, it was also fed from a much humbler source—the "goliards" or popular songs originating in the valleys of the Neckar and the Danube.

It was from this source that the music of the Minnesingers derived its individuality, its own particular vigor and its love of nature, in fact, all those elements that enabled it, after a period when it was for the most part imitative, to find its own style.

The Minnesingers, like their French counterparts the troubadours, combined the art of expression with the ideals of a way of life; their influence operated throughout the whole of the period that stretched from Barbarossa to Konradin and Rudolf I of Hapsburg (1218-1291), founder of the House of Austria. This remarkable movement represented the flowering of chivalry and portrayed most faithfully the occupations of the knight, his love for his chosen lady, his life as a warrior-at-arms, the noise and bustle of the tournament and the pleasures of the hunt. When a tune or a poem pleased her, a lady would reward the singer with the symbols of love—bouquets of roses, or a crown of roses or violets; and the Minnesingers described these with the same vivid detail as they did the heraldry on the shield or the intricacies of falconry.[56]

The most popular of the Minnesingers was Walther von der Vogelweide. He was born in Austria about 1170 and belonged to the Emperor's court. On the death of Henry VI (son of Barbarossa), himself an expert singer, Walther von der Vogelweide, richer in talent than in worldly goods, led the life of a wanderer. Only the generosity of Frederick II rescued the poet from his wretchedness and enabled him to live out the last seven years of his life free from material want. This much the Emperor owed to Walther, for not only did Walther sing of love and of nature, but he was also a true Ghibelline and lashed out at the Popes and the defects of the Church when occasion demanded. We might add that despite Henry VI's own accomplishments in music, his interest did not stay his hand when it came to imprisoning another musician, Richard Lionheart! The following two verses are typical of Walther's songs:

Under the linden tree,
edging the meadow,
there did we lie.
There you will find
the grass and the flowers
sweetly crushed.
In a vale at the edge of the wood,
tra-la-la,
gaily sang the nightingale.

87   *Satirical drawing of an animal, with the conical headdress of the Middle Ages, playing the harp.*

87

85

88 *Centaur playing the viol.*

88

If anyone should learn,
which God forbid,
that he shared my bed,
how I would blush!
What he did with me
let no one know but he and me
and a little bird,
tra-la-la,
who, let us hope, will be discreet!

There were other Minnesingers who added lustre to German literature. There was Wolfram von Eschenbach, author of *Parsifal* and *Tannhäuser;* Gottfried von Strasbourg, author of *Tristan;* and Heinrich von Meissen, nicknamed "Frauenlob" (lover of women). When von Meissen died, it is said, the ladies of Mainz, whose praises he had sung so devotedly, carried his body to the cathedral themselves, sprinkling his coffin so liberally with wine that the church was flooded.

We might add that the tournament of singers at Würzburg, which Richard Wagner recalled in *Tannhäuser,* actually took place in 1207. Wagner often makes reference to the Minnesingers and borrows many of his epic or legendary incidents from them. Every facet of German Romanticism was to delight in the rediscovery of these Middle Ages, wherein it thought it beheld its own reflection.

Although in general the lyricism that had originated south of the Loire remained a perquisite of lay courts, we do find in Austria, at the court of Archbishop Pelein at Salzburg, in the 14th century, a Minnesinger who was a man of God. He was a Benedictine monk, Hermann, though he is better known as "the Monk of Salzburg." He used to translate Latin hymns and sequences into German, although at the behest of his master he also composed a number of secular songs, including some "songs of daybreak." He also wrote songs for several voices and songs for those who loved their food! One of his compositions sings the praises of roast goose fragrant with wine. Mozart would probably have found a kindred spirit in that particular Archbishop of Salzburg!

It was not long before southern Germany and Austria became the nursery for a popular vocal art acceptable to all classes of society, including the Church. The seed that was sown then explains the great harvest of important works some centuries later on that same soil, where, to quote Brahms, "Tunes sprang up like mushrooms."

Unlike the troubadours and trouvères, the Minnesingers accompanied themselves. Their pieces were generally rather long and comprised two stanzas and an envoy. The stanzas were both sung in the same tune, and the envoy introduced a new melody.[57] The notation used was the same as that of the troubadours and of plaint-chant (square notation) or Gothic (horseshoe notation); the meter of the verse dictated the rhythm.

The Meistersingers

The art of the Minnesingers was aristocratic; the men who practiced it were largely of noble birth, or at least of good family. However, with the rise of the bourgeoisie and the merchant class at the beginning of the 14th century, the art went into decline and was replaced by the *Meistersang* (Mastersong). As might be expected of merchants who kept detailed records of their fortunes and whose ledger was their Bible, they could not visualize any art without a multitude of rules and regulations! They organized their music as they organized their great corporations, abandoning the realm of free imagination to the pedants. They opened a singing school at Mainz which became, and remained, the center of the movement. Strasbourg, Frankfurt and Würzburg were among the first towns of the Empire to do likewise. Their first concern was to draw up a set of articles for their schools—there could be no bourgeois without his statutes! The members were classified according to their knowledge of tablature. "He who does not

89 *A Minnesinger and his lady. The "Minnedienst" was the homage rendered to the lady. The lyricism of the Minnesingers conjures up the most vivid pictures—the crowns of roses and violets which symbolized love; the smallest details of the harness; the devices on the shield, and the intricate details of falconry.*

90 *Walter von de Vogelweide, the most famous of the Minnesingers. He sang of love and of nature, and, as a Ghibelline, he castigated the Popes.*

91 *Ulrich von Lichenstein, another famous Minnesinger.*

92 *Minnesinger Reinmar le Veilleur.*

93 *Minnesingers with viol and German flute.*

yet know the tablature is a novice; he who knows several tunes, five or six, say, is a singer; anyone who has composed words for a given tune is a poet; and he who invents a tune shall be called a 'master'." The word "tablature" usually means a musical score for keyboard or strings. Figures or letters indicated the position of the notes on the handle or keyboard. Here the word means "the general rules." It will be seen that the same melody was used for different texts. This was nothing new.

Names were given to tunes to distinguish them one from another. Hans Sachs "found" such a beautiful tune that it was christened "The Silver Tune." In actual fact Sachs had taken the tune from Hermannus Contractus of Reichenau; and Luther used it later on in the choral composition "Our God Is a Defense and Tower" (there have been a number of versions of this in the English language, but there has never been any unanimity about them). The names given to tunes were fre-quently rather odd: red, blue, green, blood-tune, tailed-monkey tune; others were quite as strange.[58]

The slow, regular rhythm of the Meistersingers was to prove the inspiration for the Protestant chorales which came later.

Richard Wagner returned to old German mythology to find the inspiration that he felt the world needed, and as a result of his works, Hans Sachs, who lived from 1494 to 1576, has become for us the very prototype of the Meistersinger. He was not the only one to secure a place in history, however. Along with him, Hans Volz and Hans Rosen-plüt deserve to be remembered.

The art of the Meistersingers maintained the tradition of the Minnesingers, as well as their ideal of monody, beyond the 15th century, though not without a certain amount of pedantry. New forms of expression had long since developed and music had been diverted, with the advent of polyphony, into most unsuspected paths, as we shall see.

94 *Otto IV of Brandenburg. The chessboard probably symbolizes
the love game of the "Minne" (courtly love). In the foreground,
musicians with trumpets, drums and bagpipes.*

95 *Minnesinger Heinrich Frauenlob, clad in the costume of
the "King of Minstrels." At his feet, an ensemble with the favorite
instruments of the time—drums, flutes with bellows, reed pipes,
crotta, psaltery, bagpipes, viol.*

96 The Joy of Love. *"Did he kiss me? A thousand times!
See my mouth is yet red from his kisses!"
(Walter von der Vogelweide.)*

97-98 *Musical chords and modes—strange symbols in a treatise by Boethius. This philosopher based his musical theories on the symbolism of Pythagorian doctrine.*

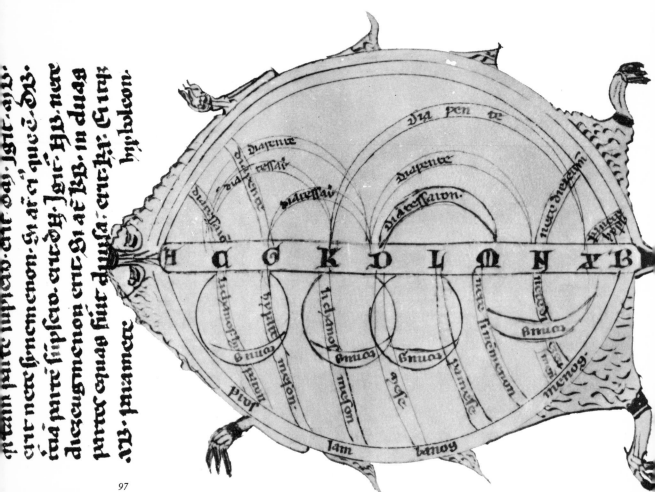

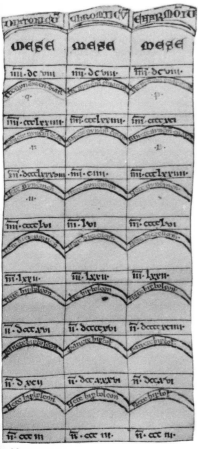

Let us suppose that some new and very powerful barbarian invasion or some natural cataclysm had put an end to Christianity around the year 1000. How might its music have been distinguished from that of other civilizations? On the surface, the marks would appear indistinct. Moreover, it would be outdone by even ancient Mesopotamia or China in view of their instrumental and orchestral development. If we regard Gregorian music as superior in quality to other forms of music, this is because we are much closer to it in history and all our music is based on it; there is the additional reason that we have nothing with which we can accurately compare it. Neither Egypt nor Greece left any similar collection, though future discoveries are not outside the bounds of possibility.

On the face of it, the only element that might suggest a new trend is the fact that musicians were very much concerned with finding a new and more exact system of notation. When one thinks of what music became in the interval between Perotinus, choirmaster and organist at Notre Dame de Paris at the end of the 12th century, and J.S. Bach—a mere few centuries—one is bound to ponder the why's of such a transformation. This was a short span of time compared with the thousands of years of musical culture that preceded it without any major break or any significant innovation.

Was the change due to a new awareness in man himself, as Ernest Ansermet (a conductor born at Vevey in 1883) would have it? To man's dawning realization of himself as a complete, individual entity, possessing his own means of self-determination? Ansermet thinks this was so, and that this was a feature of the West's entry onto the stage of history. He says further that this new awareness had a direct bearing on the rules and principles governing musical creation. This is why, he maintains, music is the most Western of all Western arts, just as the culture that resulted from it is specifically Western, though open to all.[59]

Or was the transformation, as Max Weber thinks, consequent upon the development of a spirit of rationalism? As a result of some inexplicable inner foresight, was it, in fact, that man wanted to create for himself an ideal world of sound, a virtual "reservoir" of spirituality from which he could draw when mere reason palled? For he stood at the threshold of an age that was to rob life of the piquancy which society had hitherto known and deliver it up to the cold genius of science.

These problems must perforce be left to philosophers.

As for the parallel often drawn between the development of polyphony and the birth of Gothic, what significance has it, even assuming that it was not merely by chance that polyphony and Gothic appeared together? No movement of ideas ever has the same meaning throughout all the arts, for the simple reason that each considers a different aspect to be the most valuable.

At all events, music, which had up to now been transmitted orally and remained more or less homophonic, was to take on a visual form, which would render it objective—the score; and the demands of accuracy would become more and more exacting. Other voices came to join the main melody in obedience to certain laws. The simultaneous sound that resulted from polyphony fostered in musicians a completely new idea, that of *harmony,* which in its turn generated its own grammar and syntax. The role of the performer, which till now had been paramount, would be diminished for the benefit of the composer, whose importance and whose demands increased more and more as it became possible to write down everything.

Music had hitherto been created on the basis of certain systems, and although these were sometimes improved upon, there was always a certain amount of improvisation. From now on, *works* would be produced in which the creator could express himself with the same facility and the same versatility as the sculptor or the painter.

99   *Illustration of tonalities.*
(probably 13th century)
100   *Following page: Title page of*
musical treatise by J. Fulgentio,
De primo Tono. *(13th century)*
101   *Following page: Copy of one*
of Boethius' tractates. For the
musicians of the Middle Ages,
music was the daughter of Arithmetic
and closely bound up with cosmic and
philosophic dreams and speculations
involving numbers. (13th century)

The consequences of this development were as far-reaching for civilization as had been, some four thousand years before, the discovery that the spoken word could be committed to writing. The credit for this achievement belongs to Western civilization. It was unique and without precedent. Outside Europe, there has been no one like J.S. Bach or Mozart.

It is curious that none of the great Eastern civilizations thought, before the end of the 19th century, of using polyphonic notation, not even the civilization of the Arabs, which had remained in contact with ours, on Spanish soil, right up to the time of the Renaissance.

Organum

Briefly, organum is the term used for the duplication of melody at a different pitch. It is described in *Musica enchiriadis* (Manual of Music), a 9th-century treatise which dealt with the problem of polyphony. For a long time the work was attributed to Hucbald, a monk of Saint-Amand, but today the author is thought to have been Ogier, possibly a native of Laon.[60] Its true significance is its detailed description of a song for two voices, written in combination, in what was still a very elementary method, called organum or diaphony.

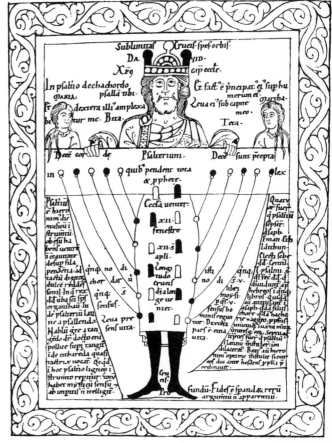

Primus modus ut tp. uersat regulari cursu. int D. æ d. utputa insuis
speciebus. æ ex licentia assumit utrinq; chordá ut uocem. Eius sc̄lodm
incipit in .a. cantus v̄. in C. ut ā Arguebat h̄. sepius aū in D. que ē eius
finalis. ut ā Ecce nom̄ dn̄i. ⁊ ā Euge sue ⁊ ā Domine dn̄s nr̄. In F. aliquā
do. ut ā Biduo uiuens. ⁊ ā Aptis thesauꝝ. ⁊ ā Domine si hic fuisses. In .a. ut
ā Beati mundo cōrde. Aliquando idem modus incipit i̅ A. graui. ut ā Domine
non est ā lius d̄s. Hoc tam̄ rarissime sit. cū scil. cū indifferens ē. habens
diatesseron superi' sic ⁊ inferi'. In Responsoriis ut R̄ Ecce appa
rebit dn̄s. ⁊ R̄ Canite tuba. De officiis. ut G Gaudete. ⁊ E Exurge quare.
Aliud ā facie̅ ē dn̄s. Aliud ā Freni sedert. Aliud ā Exclamauerit. Aliud ā Miserens.
Aliud ā Rorate cęli. Aliud ā Medita tio. e. Sal aū. ā Beata gens:
Posuisti do mine: Alla Po su isti lustus ut .p. Mirabilis
of Benedi cā do mino. Repleti sumus. eo ā Vos q̄ secuti estis me: Reuelabit
Aliud ā Dominus dabit b̄. Per Alla qui ipsius tom cognosce.

Alleluia. Alle v ia. Alle v ia.

formula eius Hęc est.

101

"Harmony is the suitable combination of two different voices," says the author of the treatise. "In the same way that if one joins letters together in any haphazard fashion one does not achieve syllables or words, in music, too, one can only join certain intervals."[61] There we have, at the very beginning, a clear statement of basic principles, which were, it would seem, not the invention of the author of the work in question, but which seem rather to confirm something that had been in practice for a long time. As luck would have it, the text is decorated with examples of diaphony, showing a double melody in octave at lower fourth and fifth and following it closely in parallel movement.

In the choice of intervals, one can detect again Greek influence. Pythagoras (he owed his knowledge perhaps to Egypt) used to teach that according to mathematics the fifth and its opposite number, the fourth, are, after the octave, the first concords. (The third was not used for a long time, since it was considered to be a discord.)

But the author did not stop there. In another chapter, he recommends in some cases that the organal voice be made more flexible. After starting in unison, he suggests it should gradually leave the melody and wait for the fourth before relinquishing the initial note, in order to follow the tune in diaphony. The end part of the singing was

103

102 Song written in neumes. From the 10th century, lines were dispensed with and the neumes were arranged in such a way that the spaces were obvious ("diastemata"—hence the term diastemic neumes). This had many important results. (Flanders—12th century)

again performed in unison. Organum is the word used to describe this procedure.

One question remains. Does the use of diaphony and organum date from the treatise *Musica enchiriadis?* If not, what is the date of its origin? Einstein points out that the Nordic peoples have an innate liking for harmony, and he wonders if the great S-shaped bronze wind instruments, from the Bronze Age, which were dug out in pairs, were used for signals performed by two voices.[62]

The Irish philosopher, Scot Erigen, in the 9th century, was acquainted with two-part singing. According to Giraldus Cambrensis (12th century), polyphonic singing had ancient roots in northern England and Wales, whence it had, perhaps, been imported from Denmark and Norway.[63] The texts are too vague to permit any categoric conclusions. All that one can say is that England, together with France, is the country whose attempts at polyphony are the most interesting. The first great collections of organa (more than 150) come from the Gothic Cathedral of Winchester, in Hampshire. Winchester was an important musical center.

It seems, on the other hand, unlikely—though this cannot be proved either—that those numerous ancient and Oriental peoples who practiced heterophony and possessed great musical ensembles were never at any time instinctively drawn to the use of

diaphony. Let us cast our minds back to the Gagaku of Japan, to the Javanese Gamelan and to the great orchestras of Babylon. The great Roman orchestras and the gigantic hydraulic organs, which were to be heard in the Roman circus, under the Empire, must have been a throwback to these ancient customs, which were thus handed on to the Christian West. It is probable that the tradition was maintained right up to the time of the instrumentalists at Reichenau, thanks to wandering musicians about whom history can tell us nothing since nothing concrete has survived. This much, however, we do know. Their activities were very much appreciated by the rank and file of society, as is evidenced (negatively from the Church's point of view!) by the frequency of the warnings issued against them by Church leaders.

Finally, certain wind instruments, together with other stringed instruments, often supported by harps, bells, viols and a number of other instruments, must by their very nature have led instinctively to the use of simple forms of harmony and polyphony or mixed melody. We must not forget that some of these instruments had been in use for thousands of years.

Marc Pincherle reminds us that although today *organum* is not considered a derivation of "organ," the fact remains that "medieval organs sounded

nur me a alleura alle luia

nnes qui in xpo baptizati es tis cristum induistis alleluia

quasi modo geniti infantes alleluia

racionabiles sine dolo Lac concupiscite alleluia alleluia al

leluia. Exultate deo evovae. ue luia

Post dies oc to ianuis clausis stetit ihesus inme dio

discipulorum suorum et dixit pax uobis. ueluia.

Pascha nrm. ngelus dni. Mitte manum tuam et

cognosce loca clauory alleluia et noli esse incredulus sed fide

lis alleluia alleluia. ue luia

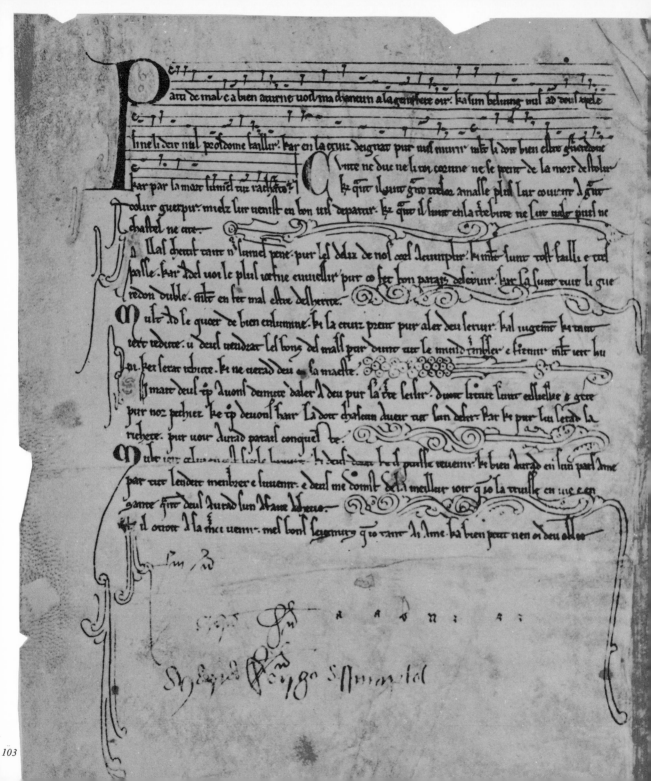

103 Crusade song, the planhs, or lament. In the planhs the troubadour would tell of the death of an important person or a friend. Notice the appearance of the stave on the document reproduced here. (12th century manuscript)
104 Piper. (13th century)

104

the same successions of parallel notes in the same way as modern organs do in some works." He adds: "Each level—the equivalent of our stop—controlled not just one note, but several, arranged in fifths and in octaves. In the great organ at Winchester, England, built around 950 (it had four hundred pipes, twenty-six bellows worked by seventy men, and two organists strapped to a keyboard with twenty stops, according to the monk Wulstan), a single lever set in vibration ten pipes all sounding fifths and octaves at once, echoing each other and superimposed on each other. This was an exceptional instrument, powerful, barbaric. . . ."[64] The organ could be heard in every corner of the city. The first time it was played women fainted at the sound.[65]

The real importance of *Musica enchiriadis* is, then, as follows: For the first time a method that was in all probability instinctive, and perhaps very old indeed, enters upon the sphere of reasoning awareness and for the first time will be subjected to notation. Let us remember that the treatise included examples with notation. As a result, this instinctive and ancient practice was to become the object of critical thought.

Throughout the whole of Mediterranean and Oriental Antiquity music gave rise to wonderful meditations, which benefited its theory rather than its performance. The Western spirit, however, was not much given to metaphysics; the bent in the West was essentially toward organization and dogmatics, and it was to busy itself with techniques. Music would prove one of the spheres in which this turn of mind would find much to do. And the treatise we have spoken of was the first evidence of this.

It can be safely said that no present-day historian of music would omit to mention this work. Yet its appearance was not hailed as a revolutionary event. Neither those who were alive at the time, nor those who followed, felt very deeply about it, and there was no further development for two hundred years!

Guido d'Arezzo, in the 9th century, had to be born before we find any further mention of organum, and even then we see that the process had not evolved in the slightest degree. Guido himself was not particularly enthusiastic about *Musica enchiriadis* either, any more than was his contemporary, Jean Cotton, although Cotton in one of his works does condescend to make a "brief" reference to it.

This reference, Cotton wrote, was "to satisfy the reader's curiosity," but he refrained from giving any examples for fear of boring the reader. His conclusions on the subject of diaphony—"Some do

105

it this way, others do it another way"—are vague and almost contemptuous.[66] This lack of interest (Chailley calls it "this obvious disfavor") is usually ascribed to the fact that diaphony was not understood. Could it not, however, have been due to that repugnance which scholars and theorists felt toward the introduction of instruments into religious vocal music, something they associated with common minstrels? In other words, was it not the humble origin of diaphony that shocked them, rather than its novelty? The question is worth examination —all the more so since after a slow period of preparation and "conditioning," we shall find that when polyphony began in earnest, it was St. Martial at Limoges, Fleury, Tours and Fécamp that were the active and decisive centers. "Now it was at Fécamp that Abbot William of Dijon had founded the first confraternity of musicians and singers, and it is precisely in the Manuscripts from St. Martial that we find the earliest drawings of these musicians."[67]

One must mention, too, the recent research of the German musicologist Walter Krüger into the subject of the performance of primitive organum. His research upset all traditional ideas on the matter.[68] According to him—and this is his most revolutionary statement—organum was not performed note against note, uniformly and without rhythmic differences, as was generally thought. The notation fixed only the general structure, which was "completed, according to certain rules, by a miscellaneous collection of instruments." In other words, the notation was merely a guide to remind the players of the line of a melody on which they were to execute their embellishments. The "play of bells" and the organ in particular could be used. It is worthwhile to pursue Krüger's research further and to examine it more closely.

The Descant

About the end of the 9th century, Fleury and Chartres saw the development of a principle that really was to liberate polyphony and to rescue it from the simple heterophony which had held it captive. This principle would enable polyphony to take a decisive lead, by rejecting the idea of parallelism which had so far enslaved it.

Parallelism is the principle of "contrary movement," which allows one voice to rise while the other goes down, or vice versa. In addition, the organal voice is placed above the principal voice and is called a descant. The interval was, at first, still fourths, fifths or octaves, but between the supporting chords they developed freely. Quite soon, moreover, this procedure was codified into movements that were permissible and those that were

105 Trumpet players. (Apocalypse—
12th century manuscript)
106 Angel playing the trumpet.
(Apocalypse—12th century manuscript)

106

not. As early as the beginning of the 13th century these rules can be found set out in a tract called *Discantus positio vulgaris*. The rules enabled choristers to improvise descant without reference to a score.

The Drone or Faux-Bourdon

One kind of descant that probably goes back to the 12th century is generally thought to have been developed in England. This is known as the drone or faux-bourdon, or false base. It was written at the lower third of the melody, but was actually played an octave higher, which explains, incidentally, the origin of its name. It was characterized by its use of a succession of parallel thirds. Since it was usually performed in three parts, an upper parallel third was added to the melody.

It would seem, then, that it is to England that music owes the introduction of the third as a chord. From remote times, moreover, that country had known a particular kind of two-part singing (*cantus gemellus* or "twin-song"), which progressed through parallel thirds. This is believed by some people to have come from Scandinavia. The Vikings, who were established in Scotland and England in the 9th century, would have taught the local population this kind of singing.[69]

Vocalized Organum

There was to be one more development at the beginning of the 9th century at St. Martial de Limoges, which had continued to be one of the most prolific centers of many-voiced music. This was the *organum fleuri* or vocalized organum, wherein the second voice embroidered and graced each note of the main tune. To allow time for this, the principal voice had to be extended, and it became the *cantus firmus,* or fixed melody or tenor, in other words, the *support* of the descant. With this development, we shall now see as we come to Leoninus and Perotinus, the way is clear for everything to be put to great effect.

The Conductus

After two part-sound, the descant and the organum fleuri, it was the conductus that opened up wide perspectives for musical invention and helped it to a fuller independence.

The conductus, which might be termed "passage work," was sung during the moments when the celebrants moved about from one place to another in the chancel. The term tells us nothing about its musical form, any more than the word "passage" in literature describes a particular part.

107 *Scene from the life of Saul, showing trumpet players, portable harps, viols and bagpipes. (St. Louis psalter)*
108 *A Gradual. The Gradual contains all that part of the Mass that was sung from the lectern. (Heilbron—13th century)*

108

The essential difference between the conductus and organum fleuri lies in the origin of the main voice or cantus firmus, which was always, in organum, a Gregorian chant. This was not the case with the conductus, which used a hymn or a sacred verse, that is, a piece of free verse, in verses and lines. Moreover, the tenor did not need to be extended. The conductus therefore did not constitute an opposition with long or short notes; both voices were equal in this respect.

We must emphasize one point. The conductus was not obliged to use a given liturgical text. It was, then, a composition-for-many-voices, in which all parts were *freely* written. It is not difficult to imagine the potentialities of such an innovation.

The conductus developed independently, as we shall see, creating its own structures, and it was not long before it took to imitating and borrowing, for the tenor part, pieces of many different origins, even popular rounds in the common tongue.

The School of Notre Dame

Polyphony, or many-voiced music, was, then, a French invention. Central France especially was its cradle. The memorable innovations at St. Martial (called the "Conservatory of the Middle Ages"), at Chartres, and at Fleury were to find their ulti-

mate expansion in the works of the first great names in polyphonic music: Leoninus and Perotinus.

Already, in advance of these two masters, musical history had recorded the name of one "Master Albert of Paris." And the one piece of his that we have, a conductus for three voices, links the name of this same capital, Paris, with "A quest for the enrichment of polyphony, just as later the name of Perotinus would be linked with the writing of music for four voices."[70] All other manuscripts that mention Master Albert are for one or two voices only.

The author concluded: "There is in existence a volume containing four-part works like Viderunt and Sederunt, composed by Perotinus, which are full of color [by which he meant ornament] and beauty . . . and another of three-part works which are indeed greater than great, like the *Alleluia, Dies Sanctificatus,* in which we have color and beauty in abundance; and no matter who would celebrate Divine Service, if he celebrated in this way he would be using the best book we have concerning this art."

It was only at the end of the 19th century that this book from Notre Dame was identified at Florence (*Magnus liber organi,* 1898).

Other choir manuals of the French school were found in Spain, in Germany and in Scotland. None stayed in France.

111

109 The twelve old men around
the Lamb, playing the viol.
(Miniature of the Apocalypse—
Jean Andrez—13th century)

All the two-part organa of the *Magnus liber* are now attributed to Leoninus, but only by supposition.[71] The organa for three and four voices in the same volume are ascribed to Perotinus, several of them with certainty. There are several hundred of these works (organa and conductus) from the Perotinus school, and we are not able to determine exactly the share which the master himself took in these.

We know nothing about Leoninus. He would have been gathered to the ranks of the great anonymous had not a writer at the end of the 13th century by chance mentioned him. "Take note, too, that Master Leoninus was a composer of organa of great excellence, who produced a great book of organa for Gradual and Antiphonary in order to extend the service of God. This book was in use up to the time of the great Perotinus, who abridged it and wrote many cadenzas and phrases which were more beautiful; he was very clever at descant, better than Leoninus."

That is the sum total of our knowledge of Leoninus.

The rest deals with Perotinus. "Now this master himself, Perotinus, wrote some very lovely four-part pieces, such as *Viderunt* and *Sederunt,* full of colorful harmony. There was an even greater number of three-part works, full of dignity, like his *Alleluia posui adjutorium* and *Nativitas.* The book, or books, composed by Perotinus were in use up to the time of Robert de Sabilon in the choir of B.V.M. in Paris (Notre Dame)."

Those manuscripts that have been identified reveal Perotinus as the inventor of rhythmic notation, from which our own system has been developed.

What do we know of the man himself? Not much more, to be sure, than we know of Leoninus. Indeed, scholars have discovered some five people who *could* have been the master, with no iota of proof in favor of one or the other.

Leoninus and Perotinus were both organists; they wrote organa; and that is all the texts tell us. The term organist corresponded to no specific function. It applied as much to those who wrote organa as to those who sang them. It could also mean one who played the organ, but at the time in question that instrument was still a rarity in churches.

In spite of our ignorance about Leoninus and Perotinus, however, there is no doubt at all about the strong influence of the Notre Dame school. Musicians from every corner of the known world came to Paris to drink in the genius of Perotinus and to take its lessons back with them to their own countries. At that time, Notre Dame was truly the musical center of the West.

113

114

111

112 Instrumental ensemble of the Middle Ages: organ, trumpet, viol, bells, and, played by the king himself, the harp.

Organum had developed enormously since the first tentative efforts at St. Martial, and now it was composition with majesty and proportions of greatness. It was sung mainly during the great feasts at Christmas and Easter and at solemn ceremonies. The singers, wearing beautifully colored copes, performed in the choir. Chailley writes, "Since, as was generally the case, the texts thus set to music were *graduals* or alleluias, they were inserted into the Solemn Mass, and when one calculates that an organum by Perotinus lasted no less than twenty minutes, one can well believe that it was a veritable spiritual concert at which the faithful of the Cathedral were present."

Nothing could be more in keeping with the Gothic architecture of Notre Dame, still quite new at this time, than this unearthly counterpoint of Perotinus, whose pure, marvelously free lines unfurled their fanciful forms upon the slow syllables of the main melody; nothing could merge more happily with the light from the great windows, or the sinewy lightness of the columns, rearing upwards to the great vault, defying, as it were, all laws of weight.

Still greater freedom in the conductus allowed Perotinus to achieve in them a transparency and freedom of voices that made them masterpieces of pure counterpoint, all the more so because as yet there was no restraining harmony to confine his imagination. Each voice, by itself—not only the tenor—had its own beauty, its own meaning, its own feeling.

Considerable tribute must be paid to present-day musicology. One of its glories is that by methodical research in medieval music, into its principles of rhythm, into its rules of performance, into its notation, it has restored to us these works from the Notre Dame school. Listening to records, everyone can travel again along the road that led to polyphony. Everyone can get to know a language and a writing from which all subsequent music sprang—and on which it still feeds, like a flower drawing life from roots deep in the earth.

There is no better illustration of the way in which a taste for this music has evolved than the verdicts pronounced not long ago on Perotinus by some of the more enlightened spirits: "We know for certain that these strange compositions were played in church . . . but it is difficult for us to assess the musical value of an art like this . . . its content is so hard!" Thus writes a famous historian.

Such an opinion was by no means isolated and was in accordance with the general view. Its author (Combarieu, *History of Music*, 1920) was a man of culture and enlightenment, with great breadth of vision. He would have been mightily surprised

113   The organ at Winchester. It was built around 950. The huge organ needed 70 men to work its 26 bellows!

113

117

had he been able to foresee that forty years later Perotinus would be a neighbor of Heinrich Schütz and J. S. Bach in the displays of record stores!

Perotinus' works were almost certainly written in the early years of the 13th century, perhaps even in the closing years of the 12th. He was, therefore, a contemporary of Bernard de Ventadour, of Villehardouin, and of St. Francis of Assisi. Poets and romanticists were bringing to life some of the great figures of our European literature. Tristan, Percival (the Parsifal of Wagner), El Cid. Those who built cathedrals were going on with their grandiose plans; beneath their scaffolding, Laon and Chartres, the dome at Siena and the Tower of Pisa were launching into space the silhouettes which for centuries to come were to symbolize the very spirit of the West.

The efforts of St. Ambrose and St. Gregory, the inventions at Jumièges, St. Gall, Reichenau and St. Martial, the genius of countless anonymous musicians who preceded Leoninus and Perotinus— all these secured for music a position that is no longer in question. All the resistance of old has been vanquished. The art of sound has achieved full status.

The admirable text of St. Thomas Aquinas, who was a child when Perotinus was an old man, defines the role of music. It is evidence of the position that music was to enjoy and the fundamental importance that society would attach to it from that time on. In *Arte Musicae,* the philosopher writes:

"Music holds first place in the seven liberal arts. It is with music that the Church celebrates her struggles and her victories for God. It is music that the Saints use in their devotions and it is with music that sinners beg pardon. Music is solace to the sorrowful and courage to the brave. As Isidore, Archbishop of Seville (*ca.* 600) says in his book of Etymologies, it is a disgrace not to be able to sing; it is almost as shameful as not being able to read; for the Saints, with angels and archangels, with Thrones and Dominations and with all the heavenly hosts, fill the heavens each day with a never-ending song of glory: *Sanctus, Sanctus, Sanctus.*

"It is then clear that music is the most noble of human sciences, and each person must study it in preference to all others, for apart from music, no science has ever been bold enough to enter the portals of the Church."

114   *Kings of the Apocalypse. Arch in Church of Oloron-Sainte-Marie (Lower Pyrenees). The kings keep watch.*

Notes

1	Will Durant, The Story of Civilization.
2	Jules Combarieu, History of Music.
3-4	Quoted by Jacques Chailley, The Musical History of the Middle Ages, P.U.F.
5	Combarieu, op. cit.
6	G.Nestler, History of Music; Bertelsman, 1962.
7	Guy Bernard, The Art of Music; Seghers.
8	Cf. works of Fred Bérence on the Renaissance, Colombe.
9	Jacques Chailley.
10	A. Gastoué, Gregorian Art; Alcan.
11	Combarieu, op. cit.
12	Karl Nef, History of Music; Payot, Paris.
13-14	Jacques Chailley, Forty Thousand Years of Music; Plon, Paris.
15-16	Gonzague de Reynold, The Celts; Plon, 1949.
17-19	Cf. for notation see the excellent work by A. Machabey, Musical Notation.
20	The title of this chapter is that of a valuable work by Charles-Albert Cingria.
21	The translation of the first sentence is by Remy de Gourmont.
22	J. Handschin.
23	Quoted in La Suisse, No. 5, "Forms and Colors"; Lausanne, 1945.
24-25	Charles-Albert Cingria op. cit.
26-27	Walter Salmen, The Wandering Musician During the Middle Ages in Europe; Hinnenthal.
28	A. Ott, One Thousand Years of Living Music; Munich, 1963.
29	Gonzague de Reynold, op. cit.
30	Gonzague de Reynold, The Germans; Plon, 1953.
31-32	Gonzague de Reynold, The Celts.
33	Dictionary of Christian Archaeology-Art, St. Gall (quoted by Cingria).
34	A. Ott, op. cit.
35	Gustave Cohen, The Glorious Light of the Middle Ages; E.M.F., 1943.
36-38	Jacques Chailley, The Musical History of the Middle Ages.
39	Gustave Cohen, op. cit.
40	P. Belperron, The Joy of Love; Plon, 1948.
41	A. Chottin, "Arabic Music," Gallimard Encyclopedia.
42	Jacques Chailley, op. cit.
43	P. Belperron, op. cit.
44	Will Durant, op. cit.
45	P. Belperron, op. cit.
46	From Belperron and Chailley, op. cit.
47-48	P. Belperron, op. cit.
49	Translation by J. Audiau and R. Lavaud.
50-51	Janroy, Troubadours.
52	A. Machabey, op. cit.
53-54	Charles-Albert Cingria, op. cit.
55	G. Nestler, op. cit.
56	A. Ott, op. cit.
57-58	Karl Nef, op. cit.
59	Ernest Ansermet, Foundations of Music; Baconniere, 1961.
60	Gallimard Encyclopedia.
61	Quoted from Jacques Chailley, op. cit.
62-63	Alfred Einstein, History of Music.
64	M. Pincherle, Illustrated History of Music, N.R.F., 1959.
65	G. Nestler, op. cit.
66-67	Jacques Chailley, op. cit.
68	Walter Krüger, Primitive Organum; Its True Sound Pattern; Bärenreiter.
69	V. Lederer, cf. Karl Nef, History of Music.
70-71	Jacques Chailley, op. cit.

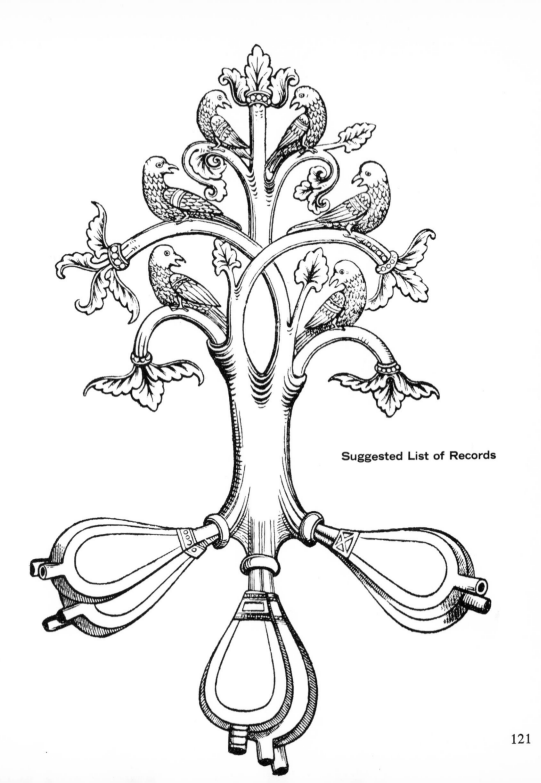

Suggested List of Records

121

Abbreviations:
A.P: Archiv Produktion
CHR: Christophorus
COL: Columbia
DEC: Decca
D.-TH: Ducretet-Thomson
HM: Harmonica Mundi
PHI: Philips
RÉS: Résonance
TEL: Telefunken

Byzantium and the Russian Orthodox Rite

In Russian cathedrals:

Choir of Saint-Jean-Damascene □ RÉS.
Russian liturgical music:

Choir of Russian Orthodox Cathedral in Paris, Dir. P. V. Spassky □ PHI.

Russian choirs (Christmas Night in Russia) Dir. F. Potorjunsky □ D.-TH.

Book of Holy Songs from the Eastern Church □ H.M.

Berg Athos Songs: dom G. Bainbridge □ H.M.

The Liturgy for Easter Night in the Russian Church: dom G. Bainbridge □ H.M.

Maria Himmelfahrt in der Ostkirche: (Assumption) Choir of monks at Chevetogne, dom G. Bainbridge □ H.M.

Chants from the old Slav liturgy, Choir of the Benedictines at Chevetogne, dom G. Bainbridge □ H.M.

Gregorian Chant

Mass XVII, Mass for the Dead, Antiphon Choir of Monks at Solesmes

People's Chorus—Mass XI with Creed III Marian Songs

Mass of the Angels and Creed III ☐ DEC.

Good Friday Office:

The Passion According to St. John, Adoration of the Cross, by the monks at Solesmes. Dir. Joseph Gajard ☐ DEC.

Mass XI, Six Major Feasts, Spiritus Domini, Viri Galilaei, by the monks at Solesmes ☐ DEC.

Acclamations and Benedictions, by the monks of Solesmes, Dir. dom. J. Gajard ☐ DEC.

Feast of Our Lady and the Immaculate Conception. All Saints and Christ the King.

Epiphany and Dedication—Vespers and Compline, by the monks at Solesmes, Dir. J. Gajard ☐ DEC.

Introits and Graduals—Christmas, Whitsuntide and Corpus Christi, Ascension and Assumption ☐ DEC.

Choral: Ascension ☐ DEC.

Corpus Christi, Good Friday, Assumption, Easter, Whitsuntide, by the monks at Solesmes ☐ DEC.

Gregorian Chant at Ligugé:
Populus Sion ☐ STUDIO.

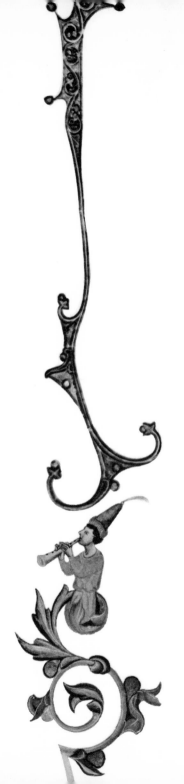

Gregorian Chant at En-Calcat: "Indico me" from the Passion ☐ STUDIO.

Plain-Chant: Christmas Cycle, School of the Fathers of the Holy Ghost, Chevilly, Dir. Lucien Deiss ☐ COL.

First Office of Christmas, by the monks at St.Martin-de-Beuron, Dir. Fr. Maurice Pfaff.

Second Office of Christmas, Easter Liturgy ☐ A.P.

Easter Liturgy, Fathers of the Holy Ghost ☐ A.P.

Solemn Prayers and Adoration of the Cross: In Feria VI Parasceve, Solemn Prayers, Benedictions, Baptismal Promises and Solemn Mass, Mass for Resurrection Sunday, Easter Liturgy, Exsultet, Alleluia, Tracts and Lauds from the Mass for Easter, Proper of the Mass for Easter, Ordinary of the Mass for Eastertide ☐ A.P.

Ad Completorium in Nativitate of our Lord Jesus Christ—Antiphons of the Blessed Virgin Mary, Third Mass of Christmas, Mass of the Assumption, Mass VIII with Creed III for Double Feasts, Short Mass with Asperges I and II—First Mass in Commemoration of All the Faithful Departed, Proper of the Mass for the Dead, Order of Burial, Solemn Procession of the Palms in Honor of Christ the King, Solemn Lauds, by the monks at St. Martin-de-Beuron, Dir. Pfaff ☐ A.P.

Compline of Cistercian Monasteries, Choir of Our Lady of the Seven Gifts ☐ CHR.

Hermannus Contractus in:
Musik im Dom zu Aachen, Dir. R. Pohl □
H.M.

Musik in der Klosterkirche at Einsiedeln in
Switzerland □ H.M.

Troubadours, Trouveres

Songs and Motets of the 13th century:

Songs of Bernard de Ventadour, Jaufré
Rudel, Guirot Riquier, etc. Pro Musica
Antiqua, Dir. S. Cape □ A.P.

Le Jeu de Robin et Marion (ca. 1283) Pro
Musica Antiqua, Dir. S. Cape □ A.P.

School of Notre-Dame

Leoninus: Organum duplum: Judaea and
Jerusalem, Pro Musica Antiqua, Dir. S.
Cape □ A.P.

Perotinus: Organum quadruplum: Sederunt
principes, Pro Musica Antiqua, Dir. S.
Cape □ A.P.

Music at Notre-Dame in Paris (ca. 1200):
Viderunt omnes-Alleluia Navtivitas Deller
Consort, London, etc. □ H.M.

Music at Notre-Dame in Paris (ca. 1200):
Sederunt principes: Deller Consort, London
etc. □ H.M.

Early Part Music and Dance tunes (ca. 1200
to Ars Nova): Ensemble, Vocal and
Instrumental, Paris. Dir. Roger Blanchard □
TEL.

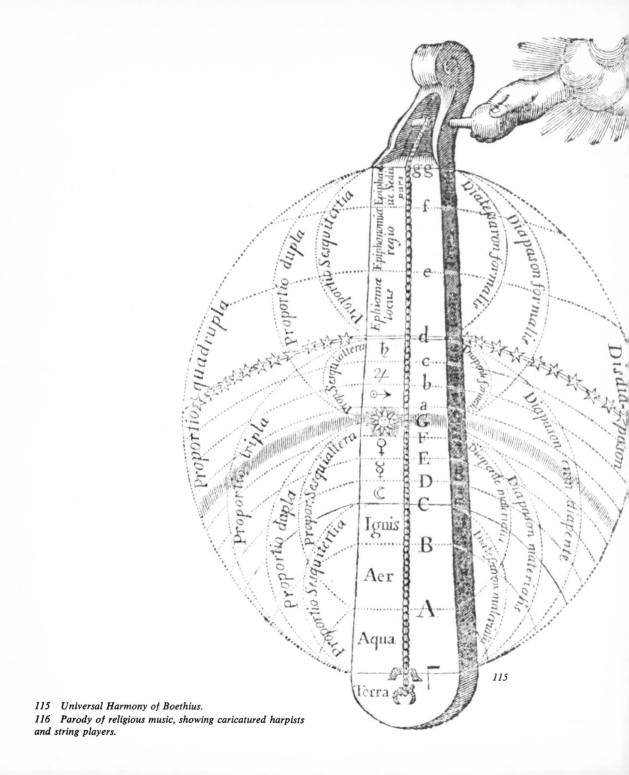

The labels within the figure:

Proportio quadrupla
Proportio dupla
Proportio Sesquitertia
Proportio dupla
Proportio tripla
Proportio dupla
Proportio Sesquialtera
Proportio Sesquitertia

Diatessaron formalis
Diapason formalis
Disdia-pason
Diapason cum diapente
Diapente naturalis
Diapason materialis
Diatessaron materialis

Epiphonia Epiphonica Sedis pars
Epiphonia locus
Ephionia regio

gg
f
e
d
c
b
a
G
F
E
D
C
B
A
Γ

♄
♃
☉
☿
♀
☽

Ignis
Aer
Aqua
Terra

115

115 *Universal Harmony of Boethius.*
116 *Parody of religious music, showing caricatured harpists and string players.*

Acknowledgments

Thanks are due to all those people and organizations that have made this work possible, especially to: Suzanne Patrick; Renate Wulff; Roger Ségalat; Wolf Strobel; Hans Ulrich Kerth; Professor André Schaeffner; Miss D. M. Moss; Radio Times Hulton Picture Library, London; National Library, Paris; Library and Museum of the Decorative Arts, Paris; Library of Heidelberg University; Bavarian State Library, Munich; Chester (England) Public Library, for research in connection with English translation.

Illustrations and documents were made available from the following public and private sources:

The National Library, Paris—figures 1, 12-18, 27-29, 35, 40, 41-43, 45, 48, 59-61, 63-66, 70, 71, 98, 101, 105-107, 109, 115, 116.

Library and Museum of Decorative Arts, Paris—fig. 20, 22, 26, 50-54, 56-57, 62.

Library, Heidelberg University—fig. 86, 89-93, 95, 96.

Bavarian State Library, Munich—fig. 31, 37, 39, 46, 47, 49, 100.

German National Museum, Nuremberg—fig. 67.

British Museum, London—fig. 9, 19, 68, 103.

Radio Times Hulton Picture Library, London—fig. 72, 73, 80-82, 99, 104.

André Schaeffner Collection, Paris—fig. 75-79.

Photographic Archives, Paris—fig. 74, 105-107, 111 and the figures not numbered on pages 123 and 124.

Boudot-Lamotte, Paris—fig. 3-6, 110.

Giraudon, Paris—fig. 1, 2, 21, 23, 24, 30, 33, 38, 102, 116.

Viollet, Paris—fig. 112.

FWU Picture Archives—fig. 85.

Hirmerverlag, Munich—fig. 7, 8, 32, 39, 44, 108.

Kerth, Munich—fig. 31, 46, 47, 49, 58, 67, 69, 86, 89-96.

que li rois

pdes uoi

ration ill

tient a li

sef dari

780.9
B959b

Southern Methodist Univ. br
780.9B959b
Byzantine and medieval music

3 2177 00865 3121